Out of the Depths

*The Experiences of Mi'kmaw Children
at the Indian Residential School at
Shubenacadie, Nova Scotia*

Aug 2000

Isabelle Knockwood
with Gillian Thomas

*Listuguj Pow-wow 2000
Dear Marijean and Scott,
Keep the healing circle strong.
Isabella Knockwood*

Roseway Publishing
Lockeport, Nova Scotia

*This book is dedicated to all former students
of the Indian Residential School
in Shubenacadie, Nova Scotia.*

Copyright © Isabelle Knockwood, 1992.
First Edition, November 1992.
Second Edition, December 1992; Second Printing, January, 1994.

This book was published with the financial assistance of the Shubenacadie Band Council, The Secretary of State for Multiculturalism and Citizenship, and the Nova Scotia Department of Tourism and Culture.

Cover design: Tanya Mars and Brenda Conroy
Cover photograph of the burning school: Russell Robinson
Design and production: Brenda Conroy and Tanya Mars
The decorative motif at the beginning of each chapter is adapted
from traditional Mi'kmaw porcupine quill designs.
Printing: Sentinel Printing Ltd., Yarmouth, Nova Scotia
Printed and bound in Canada

Canadian Cataloguing in Publication Data

Knockwood, Isabelle, 1931-

  Out of the Depths

  ISBN 0-9694180-6-X

I. Knockwood, Isabelle, 1931- 2. Micmac Indians — Education — History. 3. Indians of North America — Nova Scotia — Shubenacadie — Education — History. 4. Indians of North America — Nova Scotia — Shubenacadie — Residential schools.

  I. Thomas, Gillian, 1944- II. Title.

E99.M6K66 1992   371.97'973071635   C93-098504-4

SPELLING MI'KMAW WORDS

In 1974 Mi'kmaw writing was all but dead. About that time, Smith, a graduate student in linguistics at the University of Toro and I visited every Mi'kmaw reserve in Nova Scotia to solicit mandate to develop a new Mi'kmaw orthography. Under the sponsorship of the Micmac Association of Cultural Studies and using the latest linguistic methods, we set to work. Almost six years later and after many rewrites, we finally had an effective system.

The rules which govern the new orthography are simple and easy to learn. The necessity of having to guess is gone. There is an absolute one-to-one correspondence between letter and sound, sound and letter.

In the past, missionaries tried to develop an orthography which would adequately represent the twenty-seven or so Mi'kmaw sounds. The Rev. Silas T. Rand and Fr. Pacifique were the two most notable (the **main** interest of both was to sway Mi'kmaq to their denomination). They used the Roman alphabet in their attempts but Rand used too many letters to differentiate between the sounds and Pacifique did the opposite—he used too few. Rand's system did not become as popular as Pacifique's, perhaps because he was a Baptist at a time when the Mi'kmaq had already been gotten to by the Catholic priests. Although more popular, Pacifique's orthography was difficult to use because of his under-differentiation of sounds. This caused the reader to have to do too much guessing. Both of these men, however, contributed to the preservation of the Mi'kmaw language.

Mi'maq who were punished for speaking their language by Catholic nuns and priests at both residential and provincial schools and who, as a result, lost the use of their language, may now relearn it through the newly developed orthography.

Each Band Council must take responsibility and sponsor Mi'kmaw literacy courses to fend off the complete extinction of our language. To wait for the Catholic Church to redress the horrendous damage they perpetrated on our language and on our spirituality as well would be to wait in vain.

Remember brothers and sisters: The greater part of our spirituality is embedded in our language. That is why it was attacked with such vigour.

Bernie Francis

AKNOWLEDGEMENTS

Special thanks to Gillian Thomas. She guided me through the rough journey of writing as I led Isabelle the child out of the depths of pain into the present where I found people who would listen to my story.

Thanks to Mi'kmaw elder Peter Robinson who shared his knowledge with me throughout the seven years it took me to complete this book.

Bernie Francis, who is a Mi'kmaw linguistic consultant, kindly helped me correct the spelling of Mi'kmaw words for this new edition. Roseway Publishing and I are entirely at fault for the errors in the first edition. We regret any embarrassment he may have been caused, and we appreciate what he has been able to teach us about the spelling and translation of the Mi'kmaw words which appear in *Out of the Depths*.

I also wish to thank the following people who helped and supported me in a variety of ways: Max Basque, Martin Bernard, Anne Bishop, Katie Copage, Cynthia and Stuart Kirkpatrick, Jean Knockwood, Dr. Ross MacInnis, Heather MacMillan, Alexa McDonough, Janet Morrell, Stanley Singer, Douglas Snyde, Douglas Vaisey.

The following either provided me with information or allowed me to tape their memories of the school. Wherever possible I have provided the dates of their attendance. Nora Bernard (1945-1951), Harriet Battiste, Imelda Brooks, Georgina Denny (1950-1956), Jake Denny (1950-1957), Rita Howe (1946, couple of months, and 1948-1949), Rita Joe (1943-1948), Andrew Julian (1932-1939), Joe Julian [Seagull] (1930-1935), Margaret Julian (1938-1948), Peter Julian (1938-1947), Mary Kane (1935-1942), Bernie Knockwood (1961-1966), David Knockwood (1943-1951), Douglas Knockwood (1936-1938), Hazel Knockwood (1939-1943), Isaac Knockwood (1941-1942), Joseph Knockwood (1936-1944), Rose Knockwood ((1936-1945), Nancy Marble (1933-1937), Alice Paul (1932-1939), Betsey Paul (1936-1946), Margaret Piero (1934-1939), Freda Simon (1961-1967), Shirley Stephens (1964-1965), Matthew Thomas (1929-1935), Yvette Toney (1966).

The following kindly provided photographs for use in this book: Marion Joe, Rose Knockwood, Ellen and Peter Robinson, and the Sisters of Charity Archives. Unless credit is given, the photographers are unknown.

There are several other people who provided me with valuable information and who steered me in the right direction but who wish to remain anonymous.

To all of these people, *Wela'lioq* — Thank you.

CONTENTS

Isabelle Knockwood, age 16.

KWE'

I am holding the Talking Stick. I have been talking about the Indian Residential School in Shubenacadie for many years, and I still don't understand why the hurt and shame of seeing and hearing the cries of abused Mi'kmaw children, many of them orphans, does not go away or heal. I hope that the act of writing it down will help me and others to come up with some answers.

Our Mi'kmaw ancestors used the Talking Stick to guarantee that everyone who wanted to speak would have a chance to be heard and that they would be allowed to take as long as they needed to say what was on their minds without fear of being interrupted with questions, criticisms, lectures or scoldings, or even of being presented with solutions to their problems. An ordinary stick of any kind or size is used. Those seated in the Circle commit themselves to staying to the end, not getting up to leave or walk about because this behaviour is considered an interruption. Anyone who leaves the Circle can return and sit with the latecomers whose only role is to observe and listen. This is because they have missed some information and therefore cannot offer advice or make an informed decision. The person who has a problem or an issue to discuss holds the Talking Stick and relates everything pertaining to it especially everything they have done to solve it. After they are through, they pass the stick to the person on their left, following the sun's direction. The next person, *Nekm*, states everything they know about the problem without repeating anything that was already said. They tell what they or others have done in similar situations. They neither agree nor disagree with what others have said.

The Talking Stick goes around until it returns to the person with the problem or issue, who then acknowledges everyone present and what they have said. Sometimes the solution or answer comes as soon as everyone has spoken. Maybe the person has already thought it out, or it may come as an inspiration on the long trek back home. Or else, it could appear in the form of a vision or a dream. Dreams were a very important part of problem-solving with the First People of the land. Maybe a Spirit Guide will come, or some new information be brought to light or a series of events will fall into place . . .

INTRODUCTION

When I was first raising my children they always asked for stories. As I put them to bed, I would tell them—some fairy stories, some Bible stories—but mostly stories I'd made up about plants, animals and the earth. After they were asleep and I was alone, I would begin to scribble down everything I could remember about my own child-hood—trying through these other stories to make sense of everything that was wrong about my life at the time. Much of what I wrote down in that secret scribbler dwelt on things that had happened while I was a student at the Indian Residential School at Shubenacadie. They even took the form of assignment presentations I'd done at the school—my name and address neatly written at the top. As soon as each story was finished, I would rip it up so that no one could see it.

After my oldest children were grown up and I was widowed for the second time, I went back to the Indian Brook reserve to live. In the meantime I'd lived in Boston, in Maine and in Gold River, Nova Scotia. I started to search out stories about my mother with the idea that I might write a book about the lives of Native women, starting with her. In the course of trying to find people who'd known my mother, I ran into Betsey Paul, who'd been a student at the residential school with me nearly forty years before. We greeted each other like long-lost sisters and I taped two interviews with her. We ended up spending almost all the time talking about what we could remember of the school.

The ruined school was still standing at that time and I decided to take some pictures of it before the roof caved in. In the back of my mind was the notion that showing the pictures to former students would help trigger important memories. Every time I went up to the school, I seemed to be drawn like a magnet to the small closet under the stairs in which generations of children had been locked as a punishment for running away.

During those first two years back at Indian Brook I became more and more preoccupied with trying to understand what had happened to us all as children. Meanwhile Betsey and I spent many hours together on long walks, talking, and trying to track down our former classmates. Now I realize that as we walked and talked, going over our memories and telling each other our dreams, we were healing each other through our friendship.

I began to tape interviews with other former students, first of all on the reserve, and later at pow wows and gatherings. I showed them the pictures I had taken and all of them saw strange faces in the ruins. In one picture there seemed to be a a ghostly figure of a child hunched in the corner. Some people saw shadowy nuns, others saw Jesus's face, and others still saw ghostly animals in what remained of the school building. Nearly always, when I taped interviews with former students, they would begin to cry as they recalled their experiences at the school. One man showed me physical scars that he still bore. I began to feel that I was carrying their pain, as well as my own, around with me.

For me too the ruined school began to take on its own individual personality. Even in its derelict state it seemed menacing. I spent a lot of time up on the hill, walking around the school grounds, looking at the decayed building. It was as if I wanted it to talk to me. All the time I continued to gather material from former students and to write the first draft of my book. People who knew what I was doing kept telling me to make sure to hide "my stuff." And I did. People told me that "they" didn't want anyone to know what went on at the school, and that "they" might seize my tapes and typescripts. After all, people told me, I was living on reserve land and the government could take away my house if I offended them, or the Band Council could refuse me employment or housing if I spoke out against the priest or the nuns.

After my youngest child left home, I became a university student. I majored in Anthropology, but I also envied people who could readily express themselves in English. I enrolled in a course in Biography and Autobiography, taught by Gillian Thomas, with the idea that I could put some of the stories I knew from the oral tradition into written form. I wrote an account of my first night at the school for an assignment and Gillian asked me if I had written anything else about the school. I brought in a huge bag of typescript, and after she'd spent the weekend reading it, she suggested that I complete the book as a special course in Oral History in which I would be the only student.

The special course seemed like a good idea, especially since I regarded the work I'd done as a completed book. I really didn't want to listen when Gillian told me that the typescript I'd already spent so much time on was "raw material" and that most people wouldn't be able to make sense of it in that form. She recommended that I keep a journal in which I would write down everything I could remember about the school. She suggested writing down "I remember," and every time I got stuck, just keep writing "I remember" over and over till the memories started to flow again. I filled two huge scribblers with memories. Strangely, these stories were very much like my first secret writings after my children were in bed. But this time, I was carefully saving the stories to use in this book, not ripping them up the minute they were completed.

When I felt ready to begin, we worked out an outline for all the raw material I had collected, and I spent most of the summer of 1991 in Gillian's office working at the computer with the outline pinned to the shelf beside me. At times I would be overwhelmed by the pain of recalling events at the school and would sit in the big green armchair and cry. But, as we worked through the outline chapter by chapter, I was able to take some comfort in the idea that the book would soon be completed.

Despite the differences in our cultures and backgrounds, Gillian and I developed a working relationship which became important to both of us. There were times when our work sessions together seemed more like counselling or therapy. I would be overwhelmed with pain, then gradually after the tears and a lot of talk, we would begin to piece together words that described what I had experienced.

In all this time, the many people I interviewed never had any doubts that I would complete the book. Then, as the second draft of the book neared completion, the issue of residential schools seemed to explode in the media. Hardly a week went by without a major news story. Even as I was working on beginning the first chapter, the Canadian government issued a formal apology to Native people, and part way through the summer the Oblate order apologized, not only for the injustices carried out in the schools but for the existence of the schools themselves.

These long overdue apologies are necessary, but they can do little to mend the damage caused by the suffering of generations of Native children in the residential schools. We are only now beginning the process of healing ourselves from that suffering. I see this book as part of that beginning.

Isabelle's parents, Deodis and John Knockwood,
pose on the right with their yougest son, Noel.
On the left are Isabelle and Stephen Francis from
the Pictou Landing Reserve. Three of them are
dressed in Mi'kmaw regalia, presumably because
they were attending a ceremony. This photo was
taken about 1936.

 CHAPTER 1

ORIGINS

When the government established the Indian Residential School in Shubenacadie in 1929, the Mi'kmaw population had been decreasing for some time. The official census shows a Mi'kmaw population of just over 2000 in 1934. Despite the threat to our survival as a people, we still had a language and a culture of our own. The world of Mi'kmaw language and culture from which the children were taken when they went to the Residential School had its roots in the knowledge of many generations.

When I was a little girl, one of my chores was to help the old people get settled when they came to our house to visit. They were between seventy and one hundred years old. The younger ones walked two miles through the woods from one end of the reserve to our place across the meadow. My father would be working in his *nipi'kn* [an arbour made with leafy branches]. He would take a dipper of cold spring water with him and go to meet them. First, they would greet each other with a kiss on both cheeks, then they would stop and take a nice cold drink, chat a bit, then follow my father home. Sometimes one of my brothers would go with him to carry the water and other times he carried it himself. My mother and the rest of the children would watch from our yard. When the old people came, the children were instructed to help them to sit down, and to serve them a warm drink, usually tea, which was followed by a meal. Then they took out their clay pipes and Daddy passed around tobacco. When they had something important to say, they would tap their canes on the ground or floor, and the others would stop talking and listen. Some elders would not let us touch their pipes or their canes, which they kept always close by. After they had eaten, we gathered up their dishes and they would thank us. The best part came when the old people would place their feeble hands on our heads and give us their blessing.

Then came story time.

The elders would sit in a circle and smoke their pipes. Some of them would be leaning on their canes listening to the stories. Once in a while, they'd say, *A'a!* There was much laughter, merriment, joking and reminiscing about the past. But when the sun started to set, the mood changed. The elders would be drowsy and some would be leaning on their canes with their eyes closed. Once in a while, one of them would get up and lie on the ground and take a nap. The Council Fire would be lit, a fresh cup of tea or *pitewey* [any type of warm drink] was made and pipes were refilled.

Sometimes they talked all night and throughout several days. Children were never allowed to interrupt or walk in front of the people or in between them when they were talking. *Mukk petteskuaw* we were told. The underlying meaning is, "Don't walk in front of people who are talking." This custom stems back to the old belief that everyone is a spirit and a conversation between people is a spiritual experience because they are also exchanging their most valuable possession, their word. I usually sat by my mother's knee and kept very quiet because I did not want to be told to leave. I wanted to hear all the interesting stories about my ancestors. I was listening and learning. Now, I realize that I was witnessing the Talking Stick ceremony.

Some of the elders who met at my parents' place for the Talking Stick ceremony knew the area where we lived, not as Shubenacadie, but as *Sipekne'katik* [the land of the wild potatoes]. In their youth they had travelled long distances in big birch-bark canoes, the whole family travelling with all their belongings, taking the family dog along for protection. They paddled to Dartmouth by way of the Shubenacadie Canal to the *Mi'kmawi-qospeml* [Micmac Lakes] and then down to the salt water. They often crossed over the Bay of Fundy, paddling while on their knees in the bottom of the canoes which made them less likely to tip over. There had been a Mi'kmaw settlement at Shubenacadie since ancient times, and the area was considered especially good for its salmon fishing, for the abundance of sweetgrass and for the ash tree used in basket-making. The stories we heard the elders tell referred not just to their own experiences but to those who had lived generations earlier. The elders started their stories by saying, *Sa'qewey na*, which means, "This originates in antiquity." This indicated to the listeners that what they were about to say was passed down to them through their great grandparents. So some of the legends that I and my brothers and sister heard were at least seven generations old.

The stories were ancient, and the language in which they were told was even older. According to my mother, Deodis, the Mi'kmaw language evolved from the sounds of the land, the winds and the waterfalls. As far as we know, there is no other language like it spoken anywhere else in the world.

One of the principal ways of teaching young children was through the telling of legends that embodied thousands of years of experience in living off the land. The storytellers emphasized living harmoniously with the two-legged, the four-legged, the winged ones and those that swim in the waters—all our relations. Even the plants are said to have a spirit and are our relations. When we have our sacred ceremonies, like the sweat lodge, we end it by saying, *Msit no'kmaq*, which means, "All my relations."

Our elders were the most respected members of the Mi'kmaw community. They were the mental storehouse for the genealogy of every member of the tribe. Young people who wanted to marry always consulted them to find out whether they were related or not. The custom of consulting elders is called *Weji-kluluemk*. Elders also had a vast knowledge of survival skills. They knew the seasonal cycles of edible and medicinal plants, and the migrations of animals, birds and fish, and they knew which hunting and trapping methods worked best with certain weather conditions. Mi'kmaw lore is rich with stories about how the people communicated with all these elements. The young people were educated through these stories. Children who were acting inappropriately were told a legend. Some of these were moral tales concerning appropriate action and others were lessons in survival techniques illustrated by animal behaviour.

Although the early Mi'kmaq were free of such contagious diseases as tuberculosis and syphilis, they were vulnerable to natural ills such as bone fractures, sprains, and even arthritis, so everyone knew some herbal medicine. The older ones taught the younger ones, and many times medicine and food were the same thing. People suffering from depression or grief talked to an elder who took them for a walk in the woods to find a medicine tree, a pine tree. The sufferers were instructed to lean their backs up against the tree and to stay in that position until they felt its strength running up their spines. After the healing, an offering was made to the tree in acknowledgement and appreciation. Recently I found an old photograph in the Nova Scotia Museum of one such tree—a huge pine tree which used to stand on the Indian Brook Reserve. When I showed the photograph to my brother he said, "Yes, that's the tree the people used to gather under, but the priest came and cut it down."

Traditionally we were all taught to take responsibility for the protection and nourishment of others, especially the very old, who had the wisdom and knowledge of the past, and the very young, who held the future. Older brothers and sisters were absolutely required to look after their younger siblings. When they went to the Residential School, being unable to protect their younger brothers and sisters became a source of life-long pain. Survival among the Mi'kmaq was always based on sharing. For example, people chewed food for the elders who had lost their teeth and for infants who had no teeth. Growing children were never denied food and were fed whenever they were hungry.

Women breast-fed their own babies, but when a woman had twins sometimes she didn't produce enough milk to feed both, so she gave one to another woman to nurse. This did not mean the second mother kept the child as her own, but rather a strong bonding occurred between the child, the natural mother and the wet nurse. There were no restrictions on visitation rights or the natural mother's right to take back the responsibility of raising her own child. Lorraine Sack told me, "When my father was a week old, his mother gave him up. Aunt Jane took him and breast-fed him, and he always said that although we are not really related to the Sacks he wanted us to accept them as our relatives because it was she who saved his life."

Direct eye contact was definitely not allowed between the younger and older generations. Partly this was because it can be interpreted in so many ways, including challenging authority, arrogance, hostility, belligerence, and invasion of privacy, but mostly it was because of the sexual connotations associated with eye contact. When people come to your home, you are allowed to look at their faces to see what kind of message they are bringing, whether it is sad or glad, so that you will know how to act appropriately. After that, it is considered rude to look at their eyes. At the school however, when we followed our training and avoided looking directly into the faces of the priest or the nuns, we were punished for being insolent.

Our whole family used to go into the bush together to gather basket wood, birch-bark, medicine and berries for the winter. Sometimes, we also accompanied Daddy when he went moose hunting. He would walk ahead to read the signs of animal tracks so that the family would not accidentally stumble across the trail of a mother bear with cubs or walk in the path of a moose during the rutting season. He also had to clear the trail of overhanging branches that could injure the eyes and to watch out for hornets' nests. It was he who decided where to camp at night, taking care to be close to a spring-water supply. If Daddy was hunting, we'd stay until he got a deer, which could be just overnight. But during the blueberry-picking season, we'd stay until we had our winter's supply, which could take days. Some excursions combined different types of work, such as hunting and cutting trees for winter firewood or making baskets and axe handles. Medicines and herbs were gathered anytime between spring and fall. When my brothers were very young they usually walked behind with my mother, but as they grew older, they went ahead with my father and learned the art of clearing the trail. My mother always was the last one in line and acted as a guard. We always felt safe and protected everywhere we went. After carefully selecting the campsite, my father made a frame for the lean-to out of logs which he covered with branches of trees with the leaves left on. My mother made the beds out of spruce boughs, while we kids carried the drinking water from the spring and gathered the firewood. At night, we slept in front of the campfire with the night sky overhead. Daddy would sit at one side of the lean-to and tend the fire while Mom sat on the other side with us five kids in between. Usually the youngest boy slept near Daddy and one of the girls next to Mom, whoever got there first. My parents would talk late into the night until we fell asleep and when we woke up in the morning, they were still there. It seemed to me they were guarding their children all through the night.

Deodis, my mother, had gathered much of her traditional knowledge from the people who brought her up. She was an orphan who was adopted by a couple living on the Cambridge Reserve. This was in the early part of the twentieth century and in those days, everyone had chores to do. When Deodis was about seven years old, her duty was to collect kindling for the elderly couple who lived on the hill. One night she forgot, so Aunt Sapet put a lantern on one of the branches of the old pine tree so Deodis would have light to work by. When she had an apron full of dry wood, she took it up to the old people's house. *Nsukwis* [my aunt] was sitting on a rocking chair looking out the window and waiting for her firewood. It was already dark inside when Deodis arrived. Deodis made a fire and some *pitewey*. Uncle Charlie was lying on top of the bed with his coat over his head and with his shoes still on. Deodis asked if he was sleeping and Nsukwis said that he was sick. "You better go and get Aunt Sapet and tell her to bring some *ki'kwesu'skw* [flag-root] for fever." So Deodis ran down the hill and returned with Aunt Sapet and her medicine. Aunt Sapet opened the door and stopped short. She had smelled the fever. She told Deodis to stand by the door while she uncovered Uncle Charlie's face. When she removed the coat, she saw that his face was swollen and had ugly red blotches all over it. She quickly covered up his face again and stepped back in fright. *"Lapikotewit"* [smallpox] she gasped. "It's going to kill us all." She gently but firmly pushed Deodis out the door and closed it. "I'll come back later," she called out. Once outside, Aunt Sapet explained to Deodis that there was no cure for smallpox and that it had already killed many Mi'kmaq and everyone was afraid of it because traditional aboriginal herbs did not work on this white man's disease. "But I will show you how to protect yourself with the winds."

"Always start by facing in the direction where the sun comes up. Bow to the winds that blow from that direction. Greet the Great Spirit of the wind by touching your forehead with your index finger and middle finger to clear your mind. Then touch your lips to make your words true and then touch your breast to give you a kind heart. Ask the wind to blow away the evil spirits that brought the smallpox and to protect you from getting it. Do that four times, each time facing each of the directions."

As it turned out Uncle Charlie did recover and the only visible sign that he had had smallpox was that his face was covered with large scars about as round as a dime.

My mother passed on some of her traditional knowledge to me. Like other Mi'kmaw mothers, she took care to teach us things which would keep us safe. For example, when she was walking with me in the forest, she told me to listen to my footsteps as I went along so when I retraced my steps back home I would recognize the different sounds and realize if I was going the wrong way before going too far.

When we were taken into the bush as tiny children we began learning about the environment from the cradle-board strapped to our mother's back or from sleeping and waking up in a hammock between two trees. As our mother walked along, we saw the changing landscapes. Day after day, from sunrise to sunset, in all kinds of weather, the sky, the trees, the ground, and the waters are what we saw. Upon wakening in the morning, our first sight was usually the branches and leaves silhouetted against the ever-changing sky and the last thing before the dream world took over, we saw the moon and stars and the Milky Way of the night world.

Many parents recognized that their children would need other kinds of knowledge to get along in the white world. My father, John Knockwood, who was also known as John Sapatis (John the Baptist), had never attended school, but had taught himself to read and write by reading the *Halifax Herald* from cover-to-cover every week. He'd buy the paper at the City Market every Friday after selling baskets, axe handles and herbal medicines—he had to keep the herbal medicines under the table because their sale was illegal and he was risking arrest by selling them. When he came across words he didn't understand in his newspaper he would ask the non-Native customers to explain, and so gradually he learned to read and write English. Deodis was also self-taught, although she used to tell me that she had a grade four education. When she was seven years old, she had been sent to a Kentville public school where she was called a "squaw," stoned and chased home to the reserve every day. One day, instead of running, she turned on her tormentors and beat them up. She scratched, kicked and bit, and gave them the "dead man's grip," by which she meant she refused to let go of the handful of hair she had grabbed. Consequently, she was expelled. Aunt Sabet told her, "You may stay home now, because you went to school for four days." To Deodis, this meant that she was in grade four. She was very proud that she had taught herself to sign her name and to make out a grocery list.

In any Mi'kmaw family the worst act a child could commit was to endanger the lives of the younger children. Once, for example, all five of us jumped on the bumper of a moving car. Some white people had come to our house to buy baskets and when they drove away, we went joy-riding on their bumper. As a punishment, we were switched. It was believed that the bushes have a spirit and were good medicine. Now you're going to get your "medicine," we were told. The sting was remembered for a long time. Doug Knockwood remembers one occasion when he received his "medicine" from a birch switch:

> My mother and grandfather and uncle were very traditional people and had a different way of correcting and teaching me which was by talking to me and by using switches on the ankles. That switch on the ankles taught me more than getting a belt across the ass because when my mother had to resort to the switch, I knew that I had done something very serious, like the time I ran away when Mom was home alone. She came three miles after me with a little birch switch. Every couple hundred feet she would ask, "Are you going to run away again?" And I'd say, "No." Then I'd get a whip across the ankles and I'd step dance for a little while.

The highest reward was to be praised by *Saqmawinu* at a public gathering. That is when an elder stands up before the whole community and tells what you have done to benefit everyone. Earning an eagle feather is a great honour because it proves that you have received public recognition for something done for the community and not for yourself. The eagle feather symbolizes high ideals because it comes from a bird that flies higher than any other bird and comes closest to the source of life's energy which is the sun.

Those who established the Indian Residential Schools across Canada regarded all we had learned from our parents and grandparents with contempt and hatred. As Bernie Knockwood sees it: "They were making a value judgement based on white middle-class values. Looking at it from the Native perspective—even though you were hungry and dirty, you knew that you were being loved because when there was food, you were the first one to be fed." Although his grandparents reared him in poverty, Bernie still remembers their pride and their dignity:

> One of the things I remember is when I used to go picking sweetgrass with my grandmother. She used it in her fancy

baskets. I always have a braid in my room which I use for smudging [using the smoke for cleansing] and which reminds me of my grandmother. Whenever I went to my grandparents' house, the first thing that I noticed was the aroma of sweetgrass. I can remember in Parrsborough, my grandmother would take one side of the street and I'd take the other and we'd go door-to-door trying to sell baskets. On good days, if we sold our baskets, we'd buy a bus ticket and food and we'd go visit my grandmother's friend. She lived on the end of this fairly long driveway. Off on the left, there was a small marsh with a freshwater stream which would flood when the tide came in. Before the bus came in, we'd spend a good part of the afternoon picking sweetgrass. Back on the bus home, people would make rude comments about the stink from the sweetgrass. My grandmother, who was just a tiny woman, would just sit there with her head held high and look at me and say, "Don't listen to them *Kwi's* [son]." To this day, I can still hear her. Other times, we'd be walking on that road after dark because we never sold a basket. We'd walk all the way and get back around twelve o'clock. Gramp would be waiting for us near the spring with a lantern.

Bernie's grandfather made axe handles to sell in neighbouring towns:

From the time he gathered the wood and made the handles, it took three weeks of hard work. That's working day-in and day-out, sometimes all night. And those axe handles were just as smooth with no knots and just as straight. I remember sitting there and him showing me how to "glass" them and sand them with sand paper. I felt proud for what I could do. It wasn't much but I felt that anything I could do was a help ... In the morning, he'd hitchhike into Parrsborough. And I would sit up on the hill and watch for the Acadian Lines bus. If it stopped, it meant that Gramp sold his axe handles but if it didn't stop, I would go down to that spring with the lantern and I'd see him coming through the dark. I'd run down and

take the handles and we'd go home. And we'd be talking all
the way up. He'd tell me, "It was a rough day today. Nobody
wants handles. Tomorrow morning, I'll catch the Advocate
bus and go to Amherst and I won't come home until I sell
them all."

Part of his grandparents' devotion to him was shown in their refusal to
teach him the Mi'kmaw language:

> After work, I'd take the shavings from their work and pile
> them up against a tree for a pillow and I'd lay there in the
> sun and listen to them talk. They would always speak in
> Mi'kmaw and I couldn't understand what they were saying.
> I asked my grandmother, "Why don't you teach me how to
> speak Mi'kmaw?" And she told me, "You don't need to
> know how to speak Mi'kmaw. We know how to speak Mi'kmaw
> and all we did was starve. When you speak Mi'kmaw, you
> starve. We don't want you to starve."

Like many other Mi'kmaq who went through the residential school
system, Bernie is now beginning to reclaim part of the cultural legacy
that the school tried so hard to exterminate:

> Going to that Residential School didn't kill what was in us.
> And now we're trying to get back some semblance of what
> we were. But there's no way we can go back to do what our
> grandparents used to do because we don't want to give up
> what we have now, but what I would like to see is at least a
> large proportion of our philosophy and our way of doing
> things restored so that we will be able to incorporate it into
> our lives as a part of our core value for ourselves and our
> children and our children's children.

 CHAPTER 2

EVERYDAY LIFE AT THE SCHOOL

Dear Micmac News,

I think it's a great suggestion to write about the Resi Hell Hole. In July of 1935, when I was nine years old, I was taken there by a priest. I believe he was acting as an Indian agent in Pictou Landing.

I spent seven very frightening years there. The first few months there, all I did was cry. The more I cried, the more I was spanked and pinched by our holy nun. I had to adjust because there was no way out . . .

—Letter from Mary Kane
The Micmac News,
August 2nd, 1978.

Dear Isabelle,

The big college on the hill is gone now. Over fifty years since I spent seven years there from 1936-43. I used to always look up there remembering good and bad experiences as I passed through Shubenacadie village.

I was between the ages of six to seven years when my dad left me at this school. I was afraid seeing my dad walk away with tears in his eyes. Six other brothers and sisters were there as well. My dad was left alone with seven of us children to take care of. I was happy when Sunday came because Dad used to come to see us and bring us treats. A few of the other children seen their parents too and other children's parents must have lived too far away to get there.

There was always ninety-eighty to a hundred girls there

and on the other side of the school were about the same
amount of boys. There were locked doors between us. We
never mixed or talked to each other. I had been in the hospital before I was taken to Shubie School. I was very small and
underweight. The Sister of Charity had to feed me about six
times a day. I was too small to even go to school. I remember
being awakened every morning by the clapping of the nun's
hands . . .

> —*Personal letter to the author*
> *from a former student*
> *at the school.*

On September first, 1936, my whole family walked the five miles
from the reserve to Shubenacadie. After we had walked for about an
hour and a half we could see the big red brick building outlined
against the blue sky. My mother pointed to it and told us that we were
going to the Indian College. We walked quietly the rest of the way
until we reached the corner. My three-year-old brother Noel started to
cry and refused to take another step so Daddy picked him up and
carried him on his shoulders. Noel was too young to go to school, but
our older brother, Henry, had already attended for four years. The rest
of us, Joe, nine, Rose Anne, seven, and myself, five, were being
separated from our parents for the first time.

We walked towards the entrance and Mom took Rosie and me by
the hand to help us up the thirteen, high cement steps leading to the
door. At the top of the steps the heavy wooden doors with glass panels
stood ajar and, just as we reached the top, a priest and nun came out.
The priest extended a pale hand. From where I was standing, all I
could see was the hand and the black robes. My father took the hand
and shook it. My mother smiled stiffly and I began to sense something
wrong. My mouth filled up with spit and I felt as if I might throw up.
Suddenly I began to remember the old people's stories about black
robes and faces pale as death.

Sister Superior invited us inside and led us down a gleaming
corridor with polished floors. On the wall was a picture of a Guardian
Angel protecting a tiny girl and boy. The nun opened one of the double
doors to the chapel and my parents dipped their fingers in the holy font

The Indian Residential School at Shubenacadie, Nova Scotia

near the door. First, they crossed themselves and then blessed us kids. We stood between two rows of pews in a centre aisle that led to a small white altar with a gold cross painted on the front and mounted on a platform. The altar was covered by a white linen altar cloth embroidered with flowers, grapes and crosses. A red candle burned in the sacristy at all times, explained the Sister. "This is a sacred place," she said. If I had known then what I know today, I would have added, "And a place where a lot of children's prayers didn't get answered."

We stood admiring the art of the stations of the cross, even though there were a lot of swords and soldiers which frightened me. Then we left the chapel and went into the front parlour opposite the priest's suite. A blue-patterned rug covered the floor and lace curtains draped the windows. A bookcase filled with leather-bound books stood in one corner.

My dad sat down in an armchair and put Noel on his knee. Mom sat on the chesterfield and all the rest of the kids squeezed in beside her. Father Mackey came in and handed some papers to our mother. Mom had taught herself to read, but couldn't manage to finish the whole page, so the nun proceeded to help her. Mom signed her name and seemed pleased to have had the chance to display her writing skill, but the nun didn't notice and seemed more interested in the paper itself. She addressed my mother as "Mrs. Knockwood," and, as I listened in on the discussion, I discovered that my own name wasn't just "Isabelle" but "Isabelle Teresa Knockwood."

No sooner were the registration forms signed when Sister Mary Leonard appeared in the doorway. She was a tall buxom woman about five foot ten and weighing over two hundred pounds. She introduced herself. I could see her gold-capped teeth as she talked and smiled sweetly. She wore gold-rimmed glasses, and her eyes were blue and her pupils contracted and dilated as she spoke. When she bent down to hug me, I saw strands of blonde hair showing under her white cap and stiffly starched collar, and was surprised to see that the hair on her neck had been shaved. Her eye lashes and eyebrows were blonde also. Her chubby pink face and fingers were covered with freckles. The odour from the dye in her black robe nauseated me, but I let her hug me. She wore a strand of large wooden beads around her waist and a wooden crucifix which she let me look at. It was bigger than the palm of my hand. My first impression of Sister Mary Leonard was that she talked a lot, monopolizing the conversation and not allowing anyone to think. Mom must have read my mind for she turned suddenly toward Daddy and said, *Nuku' siktewa'lit,* which means, "She is tiring or boring me with her talking."

Mom seemed more interested in the Indian girl standing behind the nun. Her hair and eyes were dark like ours. *"Taluisin?"* she asked [What's your name?]. The girl glanced nervously toward the nun, bowed her head and mumbled, "Susan Clare." Then Mom asked, *"Tami tleyawin?"* [Where are you from?] And the girl responded, "Red Bank." The nun shifted her weight and Mom looked puzzled but didn't say anything more. She had no way of predicting that within a year's time, her own four children would be behaving in the same manner when spoken to in Mi'kmaw. Right off, Sister Mary Leonard began to explain that speaking Mi'kmaw was not permitted in the school because it held children back in the classroom in reading, pronouncing and writing English. My parents wanted their children to succeed in school and they trusted the educators.

As Sister Mary Leonard talked, she came closer and closer to my mother until she stood between us. Our parents had always taught us the social rule *Mukk petteskuaw* [the underlying meaning of which is don't walk in front of or stand between two people because it weakens the psychic bond or spirit between those who wish to be together]. Then Sister Paul of the Cross appeared in the doorway and introduced herself as the Sister-in-Charge of the boys. A slender woman, she seemed the exact physical opposite of Sister Mary Leonard. Behind her stood a boy who spoke a few words to my brother Henry. Then Henry took Joe's hand and they started walking down the long corridor towards the boys' side. Just before disappearing around the corner and going down the stairs, Joe turned around and waved to us. "Goodbye Rosie, goodbye Isabelle." We waved to him and Sister Mary Leonard told Susie to take us downstairs. "Your mother will be down to say goodbye later," she said.

Susie took my hand and we stopped to peek in the priest's dining room. A mahogany dining set with high backed chairs stood in the middle of the room which had wall-to-wall carpeting. Overhead hung a crystal chandelier. Lace curtains draped the windows and the green window blinds allowed just enough light to give a luxurious look to the room. Against the outside wall was a china cabinet filled with an assortment of gold-rimmed platters, gravy bowls and cream and sugar trays. Opposite the china cabinet was a buffet with a silver tea tray sitting on top. Years later, I found myself serving Father Mackey a three-course meal which was supervised by Sister Superior in this very room. But I never did get to eat off the fancy dishes or taste the gourmet meals that the priest enjoyed. Instead, I ate potatoes that were often rotten and rancid meat from enameled tin plates.

Susie stopped to show us the classrooms and the parlour. Down the other end of the corridor was the visiting room for the children and their parents. For the next ten years, my parents came every Sunday afternoon to visit us. Just how much those visits protected us from the physical pain inflicted by the strap I can't imagine, for it was those little ones who had no parents who suffered the most abuse.

Susie then took us down two flights of cement stairs with heavy steel railings and it was getting darker the farther down we went. Oh my God, how is Mom going to find us now? I wondered. We came to a large room called the recreation hall that had a radio hanging from the high ceiling. Large tables and benches were lined up on both sides of the room and in the centre. Along the walls, were shelves filled with an assortment of shoes, small boxes and skipping ropes. The room had a cement floor which was painted red. There were two pillars on each end and when I looked out the window, I could see it was below ground level.

The next time I saw Mom was after Susie took us outdoors. She was walking very fast down the hill with her head bowed, walking alone. Daddy was a little way ahead holding Noel's hand. This is the first time I had ever seen Mom walking alone, without one of us by her side. Had she been tricked into leaving without seeing us for the last time? I wondered. The nun took my hand and started to pump it up and down, "Wave goodbye to your mother," she said. Mom looked so strange. Her figure was silhouetted against the glimmering Shubenacadie River and she was walking away from us with her back turned. This was indeed a very bad omen! The old people say that when you dream of a person with her back turned toward you, it means separation or death. Deep inside, I knew it meant a long separation.

Our home clothes were stripped off and we were put in the tub. When we got out we were given new clothes with wide black and white vertical stripes. Much later I discovered that this was almost identical to the prison garb of the time. We were also given numbers. I was 58 and Rosie was 57. Our clothes were all marked in black India ink—our blouses, skirts, socks, underwear, towels, face-cloths— everything except the bedding had our marks on it. Next came the hair cut. Rosie lost her ringlets and we both had hair cut short over our ears and almost straight across the top with bangs. Susie carried me to the lavatory. There were child-sized sinks lined back to back with towels hanging on racks on one wall with toothbrushes on the top rack. At the end was a door leading to the bathroom with two bathtubs and two showers. There were two large mirrors on each end of the room. Susie stopped and let me look at my new self. I started to laugh because I looked so different and my sister looked different too, but she wasn't looking at me, she was trying to tie her bow on her black and white striped uniform. Then she bent down and tied her shoes, so I did the same.

I did not get lonesome till that night. My seven-year-old sister Rosie and I were put to bed, side-by-side in the little girl's dormitory. It had four rows of white iron beds neatly made up and draped with

This group was photographed on the Cambridge Reserve, around 1936, when the children were being taken to the Residential School in Shubenacadie by Indian Agent, Clarence Spinney. From l to r: Leona Copage, Mary Ellen Paul, Jean Smith, Pauline Phillips, Benjamin Morris, George Paul, Frank Paul (George's father), Isaac Phillips (Pauline's grandfather).

spreads with Mother Goose characters sewed on. We were dressed in long flannel nightdresses and tucked in before the lights clicked off. I asked my sister where Henry and Joe were, because I was lonesome and worried. She said that they were in a room like the one we were in. "It's on the opposite side of this building. I seen it when we were coming up the hill and if you look out the window, you'll see the windows where they are sleeping." We tiptoed to the open window and she lifted me up onto the windowsill so I could look out. We were four storeys up. I looked down and scared myself to death. "Don't look down, you'll get dizzy," she said. "Do you see the windows?" All I could see were window sills and bricks. The abutment obstructed my view. "No, I can't see their window." She gave me a little shove and said, "Lean out farther." By now I was leaning out so far I was hanging past my waist. She was standing inside with one hand hanging onto my ankle and the other hanging onto my nightdress which was starting to rip at the shoulder seams. "Do you see their window yet?" she asked. What I saw was a lot of marble window blocks from my upside-down position. I was starting to come out of my nightdress so

I said, "Yes, I see it." And then she hauled me back in by my ankle and nightgown. This was our secret, the first of many, and I never told anyone until now.

The dormitories were kept spotless with polished hardwood floors which were always cold. I was never warm at school. There were never enough blankets. Sometimes at night I would get up and put on my stockings. Sometimes I kept my stockings on when I went to bed. I missed my nice warm bed at home. Rosie and I had always slept together. It was always warm in our house. The fire was always going and at night I'd wake up and hear the tea kettle simmering. I missed that sound at night and I missed the sound of the clock. Sometimes I crawled into my sister's bed knowing full well that if I was caught we both would be strapped. Later, when I told Mom about the cold sheets, she explained that was the reason why so many children were bed wetters—they had a cold in their kidneys.

Bed wetting was common and punishable by humiliation and horrible beatings. I wet my bed once because I found the floor too cold to walk on and tried to hold my bladder in till morning. Poor Rosie was so scared when she found it, she tried to cover it up to save me from a beating. But the nun noticed and told Susie, my charge, to change my sheets. After that, Susie used to get me up after study hour to go to the bathroom.

One night, on my way to the bathroom, I bumped into a girl carrying a pan of boiling water for the Sister's hot water bottle. The water spilled all over my face, neck and chest. Someone ripped off my nightdress and carried me to the bathroom and splashed cold water on me. I must have fainted because the next thing I remember is being rubbed down with a yellow salve. Blisters were already forming all over. During the night, I started to cry and Rosie heard me.

"Isabelle, what's wrong?"

"My face hurts."

She jumped out of bed and led me by the hand to the windows. There was no snow on the window sill but she held her hands on the marble to cool them and told me to do the same. Then we placed our hands on my face and neck until I stopped crying and then went to bed. In the morning, Rosie had to go to Mass but I got to sleep in. She never complained about losing her sleep to look after me. She was seven and I was five.

Sometimes the little girls would get thirsty during the night and go to the bathroom for a drink of water. If they were caught, they were dragged out of the room by the hair or ear and sent back to bed, so we figured out how to get a drink without turning the light on. The water taps had been turned off, so we drank out of toilet tanks and sometimes out of the toilet bowl. Later as we grew older, we learned how to turn the taps back on and go to the bathroom in groups of three or four, then turn the taps back off after everyone had a drink.

It didn't take long to figure out the daily routine. It was so dominated by praying at every stage that one student now jokes that his knees hurt every time he thinks of his schooldays. Betsey Paul remembers:

> First thing in the morning, we were awakened by the nun's clapping. Then we'd hit the cold floor and say our morning prayers. Then we'd get ready for Mass which lasted for an hour. This was 365 days a year with no let-up.
>
> All we did was pray. We prayed so much. Prayers were going out to everybody—this bishop, that priest, this nun, that nun's father, even the Pope, and our boys overseas because the war broke out in 1939 and that's all we did—no play hardly. Before bedtime, we had to kneel on the cold floor with every window open and we just had nightgowns on.

Attendance at Mass seemed to be an obsession, and even seriously ill children were required to go. I remember boys and girls fainting during Mass, being picked off the floor, placed on the benches, revived and then made to go to communion just barely walking and pale as ghosts. Sometimes they would collapse in the pews onto the floor, hitting their faces and heads on the kneelers and prayer book holders on the way down. If a child felt faint and sat down during Mass one of the nuns would open all the windows regardless of the weather until the child woke up and the rest of us had to attend Mass shivering from the cold. We were not permitted to leave or to close the windows.

Though I adapted to having to spend so much time on my knees, the reason for doing so remained obscure. It took me a long while before I could grasp the idea of sin. I began to question whether I wanted to go to Heaven if my parents were not going to be there as well as all the Indians who were never baptized. I worried about them, but the Sister told me not to worry because God would excuse them because they didn't know. Excuses were made for everyone, except me it seemed and my parents who had conceived me in sin and who would not go to Heaven if they missed Mass on Sunday. My parents missed a lot of Masses on Sundays because we lived down the meadow, which was two miles through the woods and sometimes the meadow flooded over. I began to wonder how the priests and nuns were conceived and the Pope and all the white people. It remained a puzzle for me all through my childhood.

I felt betrayed when I was older and began to understand English and discovered that the people whom I feared the most in the whole world as a child were being called "father" and "sister" and even, "mother superior"—the very words used for those dearest to me. I was sickened by the thought that I had been calling the nun, Wikew, "Sister." We found a text in the Bible that said, "Call no man Father." But when we asked the nuns if that didn't prohibit calling the school's principal "Father" Mackey, she answered, "This is different." Even at the time I was not impressed with this reasoning.

During the first weeks and months I began to figure out how everything worked and what I had to do to stay out of trouble. In no time at all I had learned that Sister Mary Leonard, the nun in charge on the girls' side, was the most to be feared. She was known as Wikew, which means "fatty." The priest in charge and other nuns also had nicknames among the children. For some reason the boys called Sister Paul of the Cross, the nun in charge of their side, "Chico." Later, I was told that this was borrowed from a comic strip, but no one seemed to know the connection. I recently learned that my brothers and their friends called Father Mackey "Scratch." I was told that this was because he used to scrape the match to light his pipe on the seat of his pants leaving a permanent shiny spot. While writing this book I discovered that "Scratch" was one of the early nicknames used for the devil, and that seems like a more logical explanation. As well as trying to stay out of Wikew's reach I also learned to watch out for any of the "pets," girls who were singled out as the nuns' favourites, who frequently acted as their spies and who were known to us as the "squealers." It soon became clear that even if you weren't one of the pets, you were a lot safer if your parents visited the school. The children who were most often singled out for punishment were orphans or those whose parents lived too far away to come to the school. Whatever terrifying events took place during the week, Rosie and I knew that we could count on our parents walking the five miles from the reserve every Sunday.

Most other children were not so lucky. Nora Bernard was sent to the school in 1945 and she told me her memories of arriving there:

> My mother took sick and was not able to work any longer to support us, and what the Department of Indian Affairs gave Mom to support us was not enough. She still had to go to work scrubbing floors for the wealthy families of Truro because she did not have a formal education of any kind. She did not want us bumming and being cold in the little shack we lived in, so she sent four of us to the school. I know it broke her heart to send us there, but she didn't want us freezing and starving to death. I did not talk to my mother too much about this because it hurt me. But at the time I didn't know what to expect. I was ten years old. My older brother Lennie, my sisters Matilda and Leitha and myself went together. I was the oldest of the girls. I figured it was my problem to help my sisters. It was my duty to be the strong one.
>
> When we walked up those steps, I was so frightened. All I seen was all these women with black habits and the priest standing there—Father Mackey. We met the Sister who was looking after the girls' side—Sister Mary Leonard. She was a big heavy-set nun. I looked at Mom when she said she was going back home and then I looked at my sister Leitha. She said, "Mom, don't go." She didn't feel safe. But then Mom had to be strong and walk away from us. The Sister took us down to the girls' side and Leitha kept crying. I didn't notice my other sister, Matilda, too much because she was standing by on the side somewhere. But then, she started running out on the back doorsteps—maybe ten steps to reach the outdoors, the back door. When she ran up the steps, the Sister told one of the students to go after the strap. Soon as I heard the word strap, I thought, "Oh no, you're not." So when the

girl got the strap she gave it to the nun, who headed after
Matilda. I jumped on Sister Mary Leonard's back and pulled
off her veil—the whole cap. She hollered for the girls to get
me off her back. I was only trying to protect my sister
Matilda at the time because I didn't want her to be strapped.
I ran out behind Matilda who was standing there hollering at
my mother while Mom was walking down towards the village. She was going to catch the bus back to Truro. My sister
kept crying and I tried to soothe her but nothing helped.
Sister Mary Leonard put the strap away and told us to come
inside. Afterwards she was always out to get me on account
of me pulling her cap off her head that first day.

Peter Julian and his sister Teresa were sent to the school from
Antigonish County in 1938 when he was about seven. Like many other
students, his most vivid memories are of isolation and of being punished for speaking the Mi'kmaw language:

Neither me nor Teresa could speak a word of English because at home we had spoken all Indian—our native tongue.
So they started off with an interpreter who was one of the
older kids who told me if I was caught talking Indian again
I was to be beaten and that sort of put a fright into me. I had
to put out with as much English as I could and keep from
talking Indian. So inside of four or five years, I forgot all my
Indian. When I got out in '47, I knew very little of my native
tongue. I felt sort of ashamed in talking Indian. Well, just
think, it was pounded out of me with a few strappings from
the nuns. Also, I had missed a few meals every time I got
caught talking Indian.

As far as writing letters home, all our mail was cen-
sored. If there was any mention about the school, you were
taken in front of Father Mackey and given a beating. And
also were forced to tear up the letter and write another one.
You had to rewrite the whole letter with the things you had
on the first one left out. All the incoming mail was either
read by Father or the nuns.

Unknown boys eating beans and bread on Saturday night in the refectory.

Although more than fifty years have passed since their first arrival at the school, many former pupils share vivid memories of being constantly hungry. On the boys' side food was used to maintain a pecking order. Peter Julian remembers:

> In order to get a little extra from the boys, I had to turn around and take a boy's part even if I had to beat someone up. Promising to take a boy's part meant I had a little extra piece of cake on Sundays. That was a little treat. A little piece of cake or even an extra slice of bread—there was no such thing as a second helping. I'd ask one of the younger boys or one of those they picked on or they'd come right up to me and say, "If you take my part, I'll give you an extra slice of bread every day, or cake and dessert." So we made little lunch bags by sewing or knitting them together which they filled up and took

to the washroom where we went to get paid.

Later, when I started working in the barn, I stole cow food called Munchkuns which were little pieces of grain about an inch long by a quarter of an inch wide. And we stole all the milk we could drink in order to have a little extra for breakfast. For dinner, we stole all the carrots and turnips we could get a hold of. And we picked leftover food, such as chicken bones from the priest's and Sisters' garbage pails. Even though fishing was not allowed, we found a way to make jack knives from ordinary table knives which we used for cleaning the fish—nothing fancy. We made hooks from safety pins and used ordinary string for the line and rocks for sinkers. We'd throw it out like a lasso. We picked up little cans to boil our eels in and built a fire in an oil barrel to roast and fry them.

Alice Paul remembers being made to go hungry as punishment:

One day when some kid made a mistake and threw some potato peelings in the milk can, we were all punished until that person confessed. We had no meals for two days. I was ten and my sister was fourteen. She took a sandwich from the kitchen and sat me on the last hopper in the toilet room. I was so hungry. I was eating my sandwich trying not to make any noise to avoid getting caught.

Some students formed quite favourable first impressions of the school on their first day, only to be subjected to a rude awakening later on. Betsey Paul, who arrived at the school with her two older brothers just after her mother died, was one of these.

On our first day Wikew was so sweet. My God, she was as sweet as apple pie. I thought I was in heaven already she was so sweet. And my father, he said, "My goodness, you're in good hands." Good gravy, I thought I was in good hands too and that I had it made. But when my father left, I burst out into tears because I used to talk Indian—no word of English yet. I was boo-hooing so badly, *"Kitu'-l'miey"* [I want to go home].

Sister took me down to the recreation hall where they treated me good for a couple of days. Then I was one of the kids—everything started coming at me and I had to be treated like one of the children after that. Talk about misery! I'm telling you. It was terrible—like prison or a concentration camp.

When I entered that school, I had a cute little coat which my father went out personally and bought. Now I had more when I went in than when I came out. Of course, I had my own underwear and this little green dress which was beautiful and which I loved so much with a cute little hat and shoes to go with it. Now when I came out, all they gave me was one thin dress, a little slip and panties and funny looking old shoes—old ladies' looking shoes and no sweater. Just enough to put over my body, that's all. Speaking about shoes now— we used to have to wear boys' scampers—we were hardly the favourites to get the new shoes. We always got hand-me-downs and that really disfigured my feet because they were so tight. You know, according to the doctors, we are not supposed to wear anybody else's shoes but we had no choice.

As a result of wearing too-tight shoes during her ten years at the school Betsey Paul's feet have grown crooked with permanently misshapen toes. Because Father Mackey never distributed all of the clothing and shoes allocated to the school by Indian Affairs, shoes that fitted became a much-coveted item among the children. About once a year, Wikew gave out new shoes to her favourites. To the rest of us, the shoeboxes became prized possessions which we filled with our valuables such as barrettes, bows, bobby pins, coloured pieces of yarn, prayer beads, medals, holy cards of all sorts, safety pins and, if you were wealthy, a picture of a movie star—any movie star would do. During her tantrums, Wikew would go around the presses where the junk boxes were kept and dump them all on the floor. Then she'd get her pets to gather up the stuff and throw it in the garbage and the process of gathering valuables would start over. Empty Moir's Pot of Gold chocolate boxes from the nuns were also a prized possession. Even though we never got a taste of the chocolates, it was good to smell the chocolate scent on the inside cover which lingered for several days. Rita Joe, a Mi'kmaw poet, also remembers prizing special objects:

> No, I never had a junk box—never. But if I got a hold of a comb, or two or three bobby pins, or a pin which somebody gave me, I would treasure it, holding onto it as much as possible. It meant junk but if you don't have anybody, anything, it was a treasure. I hate to remember those bad stories, I like to dwell on the good ones.

Even those of us with families who lived nearby were sometimes not permitted to go home at Christmas. But it was the one day in the school year when we were allowed to be with our brothers and sisters. On Christmas morning, we'd get our presents from home and get to sit with our brothers and sisters. There would be a lot of clowning around because brothers and sisters wanted to reassure themselves by making some kind of physical contact. Little girls would rumple their brother's hair and boys would tease their sisters. We didn't dare hug or kiss each other. The nuns always read something bad into any kind of outward display of affection.

Doug Knockwood remembers one Christmas at the school:

> My dad came down with Christmas gifts for me and my brother Ralph and when he saw us, he realized that he had made a mistake by letting us go. The nuns wouldn't allow us to have the gifts and my father had to take them back home. The only thing we were allowed to have was the candy and the fruit, so we had to eat it all before it was taken from us. Then we went down to eat Christmas dinner which we were unable to eat. One of the boys had loosened the top of the salt shaker and the whole thing spilled onto my dinner. I remember Sister Anderson stirring everything up with a spoon. Then she grabbed a handful of my hair and tilted my head back. Then she shovelled the food in my mouth until I threw up all over my clothes. When I stopped vomiting, she tilted my head back and shovelled the rest of the food in. Then I got sick after that. I don't know what made me sick. I was in

that infirmary for I don't know how long.

We played with our toys all during vacation until Little Christmas, January 6th, when school resumed and the toys would be gathered up and packed in boxes under the tables or locked in the cloak room. Sometimes, we never saw the toys again but our dolls would be hung on nails on the walls of the recreation hall.

One day, coming down from class, we found an empty space where the dolls had been. They had disappeared! Little girls were all looking up at the empty space and blinking back tears. "Oh my God, my doll is gone. Which one was it? The pretty blonde curly one with the blue dress and a red ribbon in her hair. She used to close her eyes when I laid her down and pee in her diaper after I fed her the bottle." Betsey Paul has vivid memories of one occasion when she was deprived of her much-loved doll:

> All those dolls hung over the presses looked so beautiful. We couldn't play with them—oh no—or take them to bed with us either. We had to sneak our dolls to bed. My father came with a nice doll and cradle and Sister took it away from me. She gave it to Queenie McLeod, the school carpenter's daughter. And that's what happened to my beautiful, beautiful doll. It was an eye catcher. It landed in Queenie's hands. She lived in the middle house at the foot of the hill and she'd come up with it and I used to tell her. "You have my doll." and she'd say. "No, Sister gave it to me."
>
> We had to take all the games and toys and stick them under the long table to pack them away. And we weren't allowed to play with them except when it rained. Because we couldn't go outside, they'd let us play with them. Well, that went on until we went back to school again in January 6th or 7th. Then they'd take the toys and lock them in that closet.

Nothing more was said about the dolls until next Christmas and the process was repeated again for another year and after that another year and on and on for forty years to hundreds of Indian children. On the boys' side the identical ritual was performed, only with gun holsters, cowboy hats and hockey sticks.

It was fairly safe to ask for skates, skis, and sleds for Christmas, but there was no guarantee that they would not be taken away from you and given to one of the pets. You took your chances. The first thing you did to a new toy was to scratch your number or initials on it. Another good way was to confront the person who took it and lay on a heavy guilt trip. "That's my sled. My parents sent it to me for Christmas. You have my sled, give it back." It was extremely confusing to listen to these arguments because the other person would say, "No, it's mine. Sister gave it to me." "I'm going to tell my sister, or cousin, or brother." Sometimes a scuffle would follow with two or more girls pulling on the toy and someone ending up crying. Sometimes both girls involved had cousins and you'd have two or more extended families fighting—or even two or more reserves.

Rita Joe also remembers the tensions and disappointments of Christmastime at the school:

> I was there for four years and at Christmas, I used to hide in the bathroom and cry silently because I never received any presents. I used to envy all the children who received parcels from home. In my last year, a particular Sister who worked in the laundry gave me a present. Remember we used to peek in the key hole of the reading room where the presents were kept? And the ones who cleaned used to tell us the names of those who had parcels from home. Every year, I would ask, "Is there a parcel there for me?" No, no, never, until that last year I was told, "Your parcel is there!" I was jumping all over the place; I was so happy. It was from that nun from the laundry. It read: "To Rita from your friend." I was the happiest fifteen-year-old in the world.

Peter Julian remembers how Christmas presents were also used as a way of enforcing discipline: "As far as Christmas is concerned, a little toy, a bunch of goodies, and that was it. They gave us a certain amount of time to eat them and then the bag was taken away from you and when you were good, it was given back."

For most of us the important part about Christmas was the rare chance to spend time with our brothers or sisters. Normally we were not allowed to speak or even look at our siblings. This was frequently and bitterly recalled by the former students I talked to. Many of us had been taught to take care of our brothers and sisters; others were exceptionally close to their siblings because they came from homes where there was alcoholism or abuse. Georgina Denny remembers going to the school with her older sisters when their mother died, and weeping bitterly when they were forcibly separated from their three-year-old brother Jake. Eventually they were allowed to visit with Jake for about an hour once a month, "with the nuns walking back and forth to make sure you didn't speak Mi'kmaw." One man recalls the forced separation from his sister and the life-long effect it had on their relationship:

> I was instructed by my grandfather to watch out for my little sister. As soon as we got off the train where we held hands all the way from Springhill, we were picked up by the priest—Father Mackey. I was told to sit in the front seat, and my sister was told to sit in the back seat. When we arrived at the school, there was no one there. They were all home for vacation. I was taken to the boy's side and my sister was taken to the girls' side. We were the only ones there. At meals, we were seated at separate tables and forbidden to speak to each other. After meals, we went out to play—alone. We have never been able to get close again. Now, we're just like passing ships in the night.

Behind the refectory was a room called the scullery where dishes were washed in four deep stainless steel sinks. After breakfast, the boys washed and dried the dishes and reset the tables for dinner at noon. The scullery girls did the same after dinner and supper. In the scullery were two oblong windows with heavy wired screens which were designed to discourage any contact between girls and boys. Occasionally, a boy would risk strapping and throw a ball in the corner where the windows were. He'd tap on the window and ask if his sister was around. Girls would gather around the window and say, "Say hi to my brother or cousin. Tell this guy I like him." Then the boy would take the message and run with it back to the boys' yard with a ball in his hands and maybe a note in his pocket.

The kitchen windows led into the boys' yard too, but it was riskier to make contact there because there was always a supervising nun

Serving beans is Bridget Ann Paul.

nearby. But there were certain hours when the bell rang for all the nuns to go to prayers—all except Wikew who made her own rules and could appear or disappear at the drop of a hat. Somehow or other, somebody always knew where she was. "Where's Wikew?" "I just seen her going in the chapel, or laundry, or Sisters' dining room or wherever . . ." Then there would be a lot of scurrying around to make contact with loved ones.

One sunny afternoon I was tossing the ball over the clothesline with my friends Maimie and Rita when I saw my brother Joe peeking around the furnace wall. When I looked up I saw him watching me.

"Are you alright, Isabelle?"

"Yeah, I'm alright. You ain't supposed to be there. You'll get a strapping if *Aniap* [the nun] catches you."

"Where's Rosie?"

"She's over there playing ball."

"Is she alright?"

"Yeah, she's alright."

"Okay, okay, I just wanted to see you. Bye."

Other glimpses of our brothers were often charged with fear and tension. Three times a day we all went to the refectory, feeling hungry, feeling glad to get a chance of a glimpse of our brothers. But three times a day we went through terror that one of our brothers would be singled out for punishment. One year, my three brothers were all there at the same time. The boys would come into the refectory in a line with the little guys leading the way. The first brother I'd see would be Noel. We were very young. The girls filed in first and we would be standing by our places waiting. "Oh good, there he is, no bald head. Hair cut a little short but not bald." Then I'd hold my breath until I saw Joe. Another sigh of relief—not bald. The suspense was not over yet and I'd watch for Henry. He was the biggest worry because, being the oldest, he was more likely to run away than the younger ones. But he never ran away, much to my relief.

You should have seen the look on the faces of the sisters and cousins of the boys who walked in that refectory with bald heads. It was awful having to watch them holding back the tears and the hurt of not being able to help—or even talk to them. A lot of resentment built up over the years because we belong to a tribal society where everyone is affected by the good or bad of one. People coming from the same reserve acted like extended families at the school, so that if you picked on one reserve member, you picked on all. So if someone from your reserve had their head shaved, you became part of their shame. What made me most afraid in those years was what might be done to my brothers and sisters. I was particularly fearful that Rosie would run away because of constantly being picked on by Wikew. What hurts me most now is the memory of that terror.

Astonishingly, some children poked fun. Mom had always taught us not to laugh at the misfortunes of others because the same thing could happen to us. Sometimes a day or two would pass without incident and I would begin to relax and look forward to enjoying a meal. But then, without warning, a fellow-pupil would be paraded in front of us while we all said Grace. Sometimes it would be someone who had wet the bed and was made to stand with the wet sheet over their head. We couldn't see who it was hidden by the sheet and would all look to our brothers' and sisters' places to see if it was them. Sometimes we would also have to watch while one or both nuns strapped our brothers or sisters. Every time I had to watch someone getting beaten, I would say to myself, "But Mom will be here on Sunday." Every Sunday for ten years, rain or shine, I knew I could rely on my parents being there.

There were two closets without windows in the refectory. One was directly behind the girls' tables under the kitchen stairs. It measured about four feet wide and about eight feet long, with the bottom of the stairs cutting off the ceiling on one end. New mops and brooms were stored there. The other closet measured about ten by twelve feet and had shelves on three of its walls which held bars of soap and table-cloths and an assortment of supplies. Strong detergents and disinfectants permeated this stuffy room that had no light except a dim glow that seeped in through the crack under the door. This was the infamous room which became known to students in the 1950s as "the dungeon" and was used to punish runaway kids.

I remember when I was about thirteen, two boys ran away, got caught and were brought back. When the boys filed into the refectory on the next day, their places in line were empty. The girls used to file in first and stand in place with hands folded waiting for Grace to be said. The two nuns were in position at the boys' end of the room. Wikew looked briefly at Chico, the one in charge of the boys, and nodded. Chico started walking toward me, or so I thought. I went numb with fear because I never knew what to expect from them. When she passed my table, cold chills went up my spine and my hair stood on end. Her head was bowed slightly and her right hand was in her pocket. Wikew, I could see, stood where she had a good view of the whole room and she scrutinized everyone. Chico turned left to the first soap closet, took a key out of her pocket and unlocked the door. The room was dark. Out stepped a boy about my own age blinking his eyes. His head had been shaven bald. He wore a khaki shirt and appeared relieved to get out. He stood in front of Chico with his head down. She turned and walked back to the other closet behind the big girls' table without saying a word and did the same thing. Out stepped another boy the same age, with the same hair cut and dressed in a khaki shirt. He too blinked his eyes and stood with head bowed by the open door. Chico turned without saying a word and walked back and stood beside Wikew who said, "In the name of the Father and of the Son and of the Holy Ghost, Amen."

We said the Grace and Chico sent down two plates with a slice of bread and a tin cup of water. The bald-headed boys ate the bread and drank the water and stood holding their empty trays while the rest of us ate our meal. I felt dizzy from holding back tears and I didn't dare say anything because someone might be watching and I'd get the same! When both nuns had their backs turned, I glanced over at the boys. They were not crying. After the meal was over, Chico walked down the aisle again and locked the boys in the closets. Then she put the skeleton key back in her pocket. The procedure was repeated at suppertime and again at noon the next day.

Day after day, week after week, month after month and year after year for seven, eight, nine or ten years, this was the atmosphere we ate our meals in—an atmosphere of fear of the unknown, the unexpected, and the reality that you could be next. While not all the nuns at the school were cruel, it was profoundly confusing to us that Father Mackey and the nuns directly in charge of both girls and boys, far from being examples of Christian love and forgiveness, were for us objects of terror. What continues to mystify many of those who endured the school is the depth of some nuns' hatred for the children. When, as little girls, we tried to puzzle out why Wikew hated us so much, we came to the conclusion that she must have been sent to the school as a punishment. Some said that she had been given a choice between going to a leper colony and coming to us and that she had chosen to come to us. I don't know if we believed this or not but I do know that she was a cruel woman whom we feared and hated and who feared and hated us. We were all destined to live together for several years and neither she nor we knew how to break loose.

Girl at desk on right: Rita Bernard, others unknown.

I enjoyed pottery but we never got to keep our pots or give them away as gifts. L to R: unknown, Marion Charles, Betsey Paul, Mary Ellen Piero, nun, unknown, Mary Charles, unknown, Isabelle Knockwood, unknown.

 CHAPTER 3

WORK AND PLAY

Teachers note the following suggestions:

Language: Every effort must be made to induce pupils to speak English and to teach them to understand it. Insist on English during even the supervised play. Failure in this means wasted efforts.

Reading: Pupils must be taught to read distinctly. Inspectors report that Indian children either mumble inaudibly or shout their words in spasmodic fashion. It will be considered a proof of the incompetency of a teacher if pupils are found to read "parrot fashion," i.e. without an understanding of what they read. Pupils should understand as they read. The sentence is the unit of thought. Bend every effort to obtain intelligent reading.

Calisthenics: Exercises, frequently accompanied by singing, to afford variation during work and to improve physique. Lay stress on physical activities that will strengthen the chest and neck. Special emphasis on outdoor group games and supervised play.

Vocal music: Simple songs and hymns. The themes of the former to be interesting and patriotic. The tunes bright and cheerful.

Religious instructions: Scriptural reading, the Ten Commandments, The Lord's Prayer, The Life of Christ, etc.

Ethics: In the primary grades, instill the qualities of obedience, respect, order, neatness and cleanliness. Differentiate between right and wrong, cultivate truthful habits and a spirit of fair play. As the pupils become more

advanced, inculcate as near as possible in the order
mentioned, independence, self-respect, industry, hon-
esty, thrift, self-maintenance, citizenship and patriotism.
Discuss charity, pauperism, Indian and white life, the
evils of Indian isolation, enfranchisement. Explain the
relationship of the sexes to labour, home and public
duties, and labour as the law of existence.

Sanitation: Great care must be exercised by the teacher to
see that the schoolroom is kept thoroughly clean. The
floors should be swept daily and scrubbed frequently.
Ventilation should receive earnest attention. The air in
the schoolroom should be completely changed during
recess and at the noon hour, even in the coldest weather,
by opening of windows and doors. Spitting on the floor,
or inside the school building, should not be allowed.

General: Instruction is to be direct, the voice and blackboard the principal agents. The unnecessary use of textbooks is to be avoided. Do not classify students in advance of their ability.

—Instructions to teachers printed
on Residential School registers

My institutionalized education began with bells. The first bell rang
early in the morning calling the Sisters to prayer. The second bell rang
at nine o'clock calling us to class. Next came the welcomed recess bell
followed by the not-so-welcome one calling us back to class. The
dinner bell rang at noon and another at one o'clock summoning us to
afternoon class and then another telling us that class was over. The
eighth bell of the day was the supper one which had a different sound
because it was a smaller bell and finally, the bell calling us to Benediction. Nine bells in each day.

My first day in the classroom was an alarming experience for me.
My sister Rosie was six and I was five and we held onto each others'
hands tightly. Our brother Joe was in the same classroom. We were
not allowed to talk to him, though we kept our eyes on him just the
same. We were trying to learn and understand English, which was
completely foreign to us, and apply it to everyday life by watching

Girl at desk at right, Linda Labador, fourth in same row, David Knockwood.

others and imitating their behavior, acting through trial and error, sometimes with horrible consequences. And we were always trying to understand what made this nun so angry at the other kids in our classroom. The first three years went painfully slowly as we struggled to learn our ABC's, to count, recite, sing and play, as well as pray. All of this was either in English or Latin—both entirely new languages.

Learning in the primary grades was fun except for the dreaded pointer. We would cringe whenever it came near us, partly because we were afraid of being hit and partly because of the constant yelling which always accompanied its use. Mom never needed to yell at us at home, but at school it seemed that we were constantly yelled at for no particular reason. We spent hours and hours on pronunciation because they wanted us to get rid of our accent. Most children had great difficulty with all the "th" words because that sound doesn't exist in Mi'kmaw, so children were beaten for saying mudder and fadder instead of mother and father. Hours and hours were also spent on spelling, but the most frightening time came when the Sister said, "Take out your readers." We all knew someone was going to get beaten because it took at least four or five years to get rid of our accents and some people never did. Alice Paul who was there during the same time as me summed up her experience this way: "I had a hard time studying because I didn't know where they were coming from. I think they were so cruel and mean because they didn't study up on the environment or our culture."

I remember a nun shaking a girl by the shoulders and yelling, "Look at me, look at me," because she did not realize that direct eye contact between child and adult was considered arrogance in the Native culture. We were being forcibly disconnected from everything our parents and elders had taught us, and everything new was learned in an atmosphere of fear. Shame too was associated with learning, particularly in history and catechism where Indians were depicted in a derogatory way as savages and heathens. A picture of the Hurons scalping three missionaries was in one of the texts but was never discussed. I found it one day when I was flipping through the pages and felt confused about it. One indication I had that I was different racially from the priest, nuns, farmers and maintenance workers and their families was that we were called derogatory names such as "savage," "heathen," "pagan" and "wild Indian" by some of the nuns. Another indication came when light-skinned girls were treated differently than dark-skinned girls. Margaret Julian who was part-Mi'kmaw and part-Black seemed to be singled out for display when white visitors from the church or from the Department of Indian Affairs came. She was also the most abused child in the school. The message was loud and clear that the darker your skin was the lower in your teachers' estimation you were. I found that this was generally the case with all the teachers except the sewing Sisters.

We sang songs in honour of Christopher Columbus who discovered America. Apparently our ancestors had been "discovered" by this white man who was lost on his way to find spices. At that age, I didn't understand the concept of ancestors and thought they meant my grandfather since he and the other elders who lived on the reserve were the oldest Indians I knew. More confusingly still, we sang, "Columbus sailed across the sea and found this land for you and me," to one of the "patriotic, bright and cheerful" tunes the program of studies required. By the time I was nine years old and could understand the words I was singing, I had already been singing them for five years and liking them so it became automatic not to question them. Nothing was taught about Native philosophy or our rights to the land of our ancestors. No one told us that the Hurons shown scalping the missionaries in the textbooks wanted their children to learn and to keep their own Native spirituality and their own land.

We spent hours and hours reciting our times-tables every morning or sometimes spent the entire morning on long division. The nuns did not hesitate to come up behind children standing at the blackboard and to poke them in the ribs with the long pointer or to hit them over the knuckles while they sat writing at their desks. Sometimes the classroom punishment took the form of humiliation rather than physical pain. A pupil recalls that one nun, Skite'kmuj [the ghost], ". . . drew a donkey on the blackboard and told me I was as stupid as a donkey and a no-good-for-nothing and that I would never amount to anything in life." Ironically, this student was the only pupil who became a nun.

Peter Julian recalls that students were graded not by academic achievement but by size:

> I was doing alright until I reached grade four but to get promoted to the other class, you had to have the size. Your education didn't mean a damned thing. In the first year, I had fairly good marks. One of my teachers mentioned that I was smart enough to go into grade five which was in another room with the older students in grades six, seven and eight. But I didn't have the size so I spent three years in grade four. Then the following year I was pushed into grade five and I finished off grades six and seven in one year and finished grade eight in '47 but they wouldn't allow me to enter grade nine.

In September we stood in lines according to age and height. I was a short nine-year-old so I also stayed in grade four for three years. This was because the grade fives were assigned to the laundry, kitchen, barn and furnace and had to be able to reach the heavy machinery.

All instruction was given in the catechism method of teaching— memorizing questions and answers. "Tests" consisted of Sister announcing that this was a test. Everyone sat at their desks with folded hands and she asked individual students the questions and they answered according to the book. Written tests or exams were never given. I remember maybe one catechism test in eleven years. I never knew where I stood in relation to the other students in my grade and I had no way of knowing if I was right or wrong except to guess that the answers given by those who were beaten had to be wrong. The teachers walked silently up and down the aisles while we were doing our arithmetic, or long division, and hit those students whose answers were wrong. The rest of us just braced ourselves until she went past our desks which meant our answers were correct.

The nuns and the school principal provided us with their own version of sex education, which was that all bodily functions were dirty—dirty actions, dirty noises, dirty thoughts, dirty mouth, dirty, dirty, dirty girls. Wikew took one girl who had just started her first period into the cloakroom and asked her if she did dirty actions. The little girl said, "I don't know what dirty actions are Sister. Do you mean playing in the mud?" Wikew took the girl's hand and placed it between her legs and began moving it up and down and told her, "Now, you are doing dirty actions. Make sure you tell the priest when you go to confession."

Some girls didn't know about menstruation until it happened to them. Luckily for me, my older sister was able to explain. She told me, "You're going to bleed between your legs." My reaction was, "Okay, that figures. Around here anything can happen." Thankfully, my first menses occurred during summer vacation and I did not have to deal with Wikew, but when I got back she asked me one morning out of the blue. "When was the last time you had your period?" I told her and wondered how she knew I had started. I was so scared I got my period the very next day.

Nancy Marble recalls:

> Father Mackey asked me when I'm going with the boys and all that stuff. I didn't know what he meant you know. I was only young. And when we came back from summer vacation he asked the same questions. Do you have a boyfriend? I didn't even know what a boyfriend was. Did you go swimming with the boys? I don't know where he got that idea when there's no water up here on this reserve. Just a little brook which is no good for swimming. They accuse you of so much stuff as if they were teaching you. Even Sister

Superior was like that—asked all the bad questions. Everybody coming back from summer vacation had to go through a lot of questioning.

Misinformation was sometimes added to the obsessive interrogations. Betsey Paul remembers, "They kept talking about the stork, the big bird. I thought the stork dropped the baby right in your lap. One girl came back from summer vacation pregnant, but they got rid of her the minute they found out."

In the absence of other explanations we came up with our own strange notions of how anyone got pregnant. We thought it might happen if you used the toilet right after a boy had peed there, or maybe it came from kissing. In all of this the nuns were no help. I remember girls hitting the ball way behind the clothesline so they could chase it and kick it almost to the furnace door next to the boys' yard. One night when we were allowed out after dark, Sister Adrian was looking out of her chapel window and saw shadows running back and forth. Upon further investigation, boys and girls were found necking behind the clothesline and what a fuss was made about that! As we got older, boys made their way via the fire escapes into the girls' dormitory after the Sisters had gone to bed. The boys were caught and the girls were given stern lectures about saving themselves for their husbands. The only advice Wikew ever gave us was, "Marry your own kind."

What little sex education we had was passed from one girl to another, and sometimes that was wrong since we had no knowledge at all of human anatomy—just what we could see. The priests and Sisters wore long black habits that covered everything except their faces and hands. Adding to the mystery was the fact that they never ate in front of us and we never knew if they even used the bathroom until we discovered the Sisters' bathrooms on the third floor.

The nuns seemed to have few ideas or interest in what we might be able to do after leaving school. Sister Superior said to me, "Isabelle, we have to decide what courses you will take. So tell me, what would you like to be? A teacher? No? A nurse? Yes? Good. That's it, you're going to be a nurse." In all the years I was a student at the Indian Residential School I received no certificates, no diplomas, not even a slip of paper to indicate that I ever attended school. As far as I know this was true for all my contemporaries but one.

The school had only three classrooms and most of the ten nuns were engaged in administrative and domestic tasks rather than in teaching. Consequently classes generally had forty or more students. Much of our learning took place despite, rather than because of, the nuns' efforts. Much effort was put into punishing us for speaking Mi'kmaw, but the attempts at English-language teaching were quite rudimentary. Like everyone else, I stopped talking Mi'kmaw and became completely silent. I remember reaching for a piece of bread and the nun taking my hand and saying, "Say please may I have a piece of bread." I wanted to say, *pipnaqn,* which means bread, but the nun kept repeating, "Say bread." I did not know what she was talking about. All the while, she was holding my wrist so tight. "Say bread, Isabelle. Say bread." After that I wouldn't speak. For a long while, about three years, I kept quiet so I wouldn't be noticed. Gradually, I began to chance saying English words in front of the nuns, but I had to think long and hard before I uttered a sound because if I used my accent, I was yelled at, "Think before you speak."

I woke up one morning when I was about nine, and suddenly it felt like I was stepping out of a dark room into the light. I began to speak English with confidence. Over the years, the nuns would drop some hints about languages but would never explain fully. Skite'kmuj said, "Latin is a dead language and never changes so that if you should go to Rome to attend Mass it will be the same as it is here in Canada and you will feel like home. The language is dead because it is not spoken anymore." "Aha," I thought, "if we are not allowed to speak Mi'kmaw, it will die. So I'm juggling three languages here. I think in Mi'kmaw, talk and learn in English, and pray in Latin."

Once I had grasped this basic principle I began to find ways to learn on my own. One day the grade three teacher passed around small pocket dictionaries. My sister who was a year older than I was and very good with words told me it was a book where I could look up words. "What word do you want to look up Isabelle?" "Sugar-tit." This was the bit of sugar wrapped in a little piece of cloth our mother used to give us as a pacifier to comfort us. First we looked up sugar but could not read it too well. Then we looked up the word, tit. We giggled, but made sure we were not heard. Giggling was not permitted and if you could not explain why you giggled, you got in trouble.

After that, I spent all my spare time looking up words in my dictionary and writing them down on a sheet of paper. After I got the paper covered with words which I could not read or pronounce, I folded the paper in two, then I wet the fold with my tongue and folded the paper again and repeated the process twice. Then I tore the paper at the folds. I had eight pieces. I placed the pieces in a neat pile and folded them in half. I took a safety pin that I had found on the toilet floor and pinned the paper together. I showed it to my sister and told her that I had written a book. I treasured that book and carried it around all day in my blouse pocket and put it under my pillow at night. Eventually I forgot to take it out of my pocket and sent it to the wash. One day, I wanted to show my friend my book, but when I reached in my pocket all that remained of my precious book was a mangled spit ball.

Much of the day-to-day activity of the school revolved around manual rather than academic work. The school ran a complete farming operation supervised by two non-Natives, and worked by the male Native students ranging in ages from approximately twelve to sixteen. They rose at four o'clock in the morning to milk the cows. Certain cows gave higher quality milk, which was designated for the use of the priest and nuns. A wooden cart was used to haul the milk from the barn up the steep slope to the kitchen door in the back of the school. When it got to the kitchen the cream was mechanically separated and reserved for the Sisters and the priest while the skim milk, which was often watered down, went to the children. The barn boys got tired of drinking watered-down skim milk. They knew what the milk looked like when it left the barn in the morning and they could see it was not the same milk that was served to the children at mealtimes. One former student told me that the barn boys sometimes urinated in the milk intended for the priest and nuns as a protest. However, the nuns never found out. After breakfast, the boys fed and watered the cows, horses and pigs, then cleaned the stalls by shovelling manure and spraying the floors. The rest of the day was taken up by working in the fields, ploughing, planting, harvesting and haying or picking rocks. Every boy who had reached fourteen was sent to work in the barn for at least half the day for a period of several months at a time. Because so much time was spent in hard physical labour, few of the boys developed more than minimal educational skills. David Knockwood told me: "Upon discharge, I was not even able to fill out a job application without help. It took me several years of hard study to catch up on the three Rs and to earn my license in Electrical Engineering after I left the Resi." Another student told me: "When I came out of the Residential School, I was nine years old and still in primary. I couldn't even write my name. When I went to Halfway River School, the teacher was friendly and took me in and began teaching me my ABCs and I responded. I went from primary to grade four in two years."

Joe Julian (Seagull) was sent to the school the year after it opened. His parents were unable to feed their nine children and thought that the school would provide "a good upbringing and a good education with a little religion thrown in on the side." He remembers the heavy work and one occasion when he tried an unusual short-cut:

> I used to have to get up at four in the morning, milk the cows, clean the barn and be one step ahead of them all the time. Let me tell you about that manure pile. We had to spread manure in the fields. It was hard stuff to shovel when it was frozen. Well, I said to myself, the hell with this, I'm going to blow up this fucking manure pile. I got the idea from reading the instructions in Popular Mechanics. I worked hard and dug a hole underneath the pile. I knew I had to make a fuse and I used some string from a feed bag and soaked it with the gasoline I got from the tractor. I got a match from Mr. Cooper who used to give us cigarettes once in a while. Then I lit the fuse. It didn't go off. What happened? I took it out again and put some more gas on it and another fuse. I lit it and ran in the barn. I waited and waited. By and by I heard BANG! Levelled that whole thing. The cows all shivered—they're shaking. I peeked out the door. Oh shit, no pile! They sent me to Father Mackey. "What's this all about?" he asked. Stu Cooper told him, "That Joe Julian levelled that pile of manure." He thought that was funny but I didn't think it was funny. I got a bat on the side of the head. I never was allowed near the barn again.

From 1929 to 1956, the responsibility for fuelling the two boilers in the furnace room belonged to Indian boys aged fifteen and sixteen.

The furnace boys, like the barn boys, were allowed scant time for schooling and had to shovel by hand the entire two hundred tons of coal the school burned each year. Wilfred Michael spent most of his fifteenth year working in the furnace room and missed out on the barest essentials in education. He was older than most beginning students at the school and was sent there because both his parents had drowned. He spoke only Mi'kmaw and was sent to the boiler room to work. I used to see him during cold winter afternoons skating alone on the pond behind the school while the rest of us were in class or sewing room. In a short time, he would be called back in by one of the nuns who needed hot water for the laundry or her bath.

Peter Robinson, who took over the full-time furnace duties from the boys in 1958, said:

> I give the boys a lot of credit for the work they did. It was the boys who kept the home fires burning during the daylight hours for twenty eight years. The boys began at four in the morning when they relieved the nightwatchman and ended the day at seven in the evening. They took turns of four to six weeks and sometimes all year around to work in the boiler room. Their chores involved shovelling coal into the coalbin, then stoking the fires, cleaning the ashes from the bottom pit, and then shovelling the ashes into scuttles which were then hoisted up by a winch to be dumped outside. There were two furnaces or boilers. Pipes filled with water ran through the middle of the boiler. The water was heated by the burning coals above the pipes and smoldering ashes below. It was then stored in huge hot water tanks until ready for use. A safety pressure gauge showed when the pressure was too high. The boys were on a heavy schedule and slept on a cot behind the boilers because they were not allowed to leave in case the pressure got too high. They seldom attended classes as furnace tending was a full-time job.

The older boys who tended the furnace never went to classes except of course Sunday school. The other boys who were not working in the barn were taken out of school during the coal-shovelling season for weeks at a time until all the coal was put in the bins. Then they returned to classes only to be called out again to work in the fields spreading manure, picking rocks, harvesting vegetables or slaughtering animals. Their classroom hours were very irregular and an afternoon session once or twice a week was the average. Full-time barn and furnace boys worked fifteen hours a day, seven days a week.

The kitchen staff consisted of the Sister-in-Charge and four resident students. When a girl reached grade five, regardless of her age, she was assigned to one month of kitchen duty. Although some girls worked in the the kitchen only for the assigned month, others were more or less permanently assigned to kitchen duties. These girls spent only about five hours each week in the classroom since they had to spend the entire day in the kitchen on the three bake-days. The kitchen girls arose around five o'clock and made breakfast while everyone was still sleeping. Porridge was made in institution-size aluminum pots and stirred with large wooden spoons. Some of the girls could not reach the stoves and had to stand on wooden stools. The milk from the barn was at the back door and had to be lugged inside. For two hours the two girls worked in a frenzy to get the breakfast out for the children. The Sister-in-Charge prepared a special breakfast for the priest and nuns. After breakfast was over, the preparations for dinner began, and when that was over, the preparations for supper began.

I was twelve when I was introduced to the kitchen. I was outfitted with a green uniform with an apron and a little cap to match. The only instruction I received on my first day was, "Don't be late for Mass." That was my training. The next morning, the bell rang at five-thirty in the morning and I dressed in the dark and made my bed. Pauline Phillips was a couple of years older than me. She was my partner and was supposed to teach me. We waited on the third landing for the Kitchen Sister who came with the keys and we followed her down three flights of stairs to the kitchen. Pauline made a fire in one stove and Sister showed me how to clean the coal ashes and start a fire in the other stove. Because this was my first time, I was slow, which would make us late for Mass, which was a big sin in Wikew's eyes. We made and dished out the porridge in ten large bowls and lugged the ten-gallon milk cans left at the back door by the barn boys to the kitchen and filled ten large pitchers with skim milk. The cream and whole milk went to the Sisters' and the priest's dining rooms.

Next we sliced seventeen loaves of bread each. The knife I was

This photograph was taken to show the introduction of a bread slicer to ease the work in the kitchen. Maimie Paul is working the machine. Before the slicer came, I remember having to stand on a footstool and use a big knife to cut seventeen loaves of bread before breakfast.

using was too big for my hands and it was hard for me to get a good grip. I was also terrified of cutting my hand. I had heard of one girl who was holding a loaf the wrong way and cut off the tips of her fingers. Besides, I was standing on a shaky stool because I could not reach the breadboard. That put a double burden on Pauline who ended up doing half of my work as well as her own. After Mass two other girls joined us and we began by washing potatoes and boiling them for dinner. When they were done, the Sister gave me a pot holder and told me to help her lift them off the stove, carry them over to the sink and drain them. I could not lift them off the stove. They were too heavy, so she had another girl help her instead. But I had to carry them to the sink and lift them to a height of three feet. I was not tall enough or strong enough to lift the pot and the Sister started yelling at me because she was afraid I'd drop it and burn her. So after a struggle I managed to get the pot on the edge of the sink. Then she lifted the lid and the steam hit my face. I ducked my head and the pot of potatoes slipped. Boiling water spilled over my clothing and shoes. I took off my shoes and could see that blisters had started to form right away. I started to cry. I was sent to the infirmary, bandaged up and sent back. Wikew said I was faking a limp to get out of my kitchen chores, but the kitchen Sister told her that I was no good to her and to send someone else in my place.

A year later I was back in the kitchen. I was very good at making sultana cakes and double-layer cakes topped high with whipped cream for Father Mackey and the Sisters. But we were not allowed to lick the spoon. One day, I was sent to the sweet room. There were barrels of jam—blueberry and strawberry—honey, maple syrup, peanut butter, and butterscotch. Seventh Heaven! I was overwhelmed with sweetness though I can't even remember tasting it. I hope I did.

Nora Bernard recalls:

> We served a month in the kitchen. I didn't mind going to Mass because it was a break away from the kitchen area. If it was bake-day, I had to make sure that my bread was all mixed and the batter for the cookies or cakes was all ready. After church I'd rush down and punch the bread, then off to breakfast I'd go, after which I'd run and pan the bread. The other girls were hurrying to peel the potatoes and vegetables—

we had a peeler there at that time. Lots of times, we didn't have enough food for those children to eat. The food was alright except sometimes the porridge soured and made the children gag. The bread was soggy from too much molasses but you had to eat it. Around three o'clock we took a break and a shower and maybe a walk in the fresh air for an hour, then back to get supper ready for two hundred kids, ten or twelve Sisters and the priest who sometimes had guests.

As a kitchen girl, I had access to the walk-in Kelvinator where all the meat and fish was kept. I was hungry even though I was working where all the food was because we were not allowed to eat any of it. Sister Charles Borromeo was the kitchen nun who never left the place except for that one time. I went to the Kelvinator and sliced off a big chunk for myself. I thought the Sisters were all gone. Ha, ha. When I came out, I was tucking a big fat piece of bologna in my bloomer leg when, jeez, I looked down there was this nun's habit and I followed it up and saw the face—Sister Charles Borromeo! She marched me right in the refectory to Sister Justinian who took me up this aisle where all the kids could see. She was trying to humiliate and embarrass me I guess. She held a tin plate up high so I could barely reach it and said, "Dig out what you have in your bloomer leg and put it on this plate." So I dug out this piece of bologna and I threw it on the tin plate. I had to stand there and eat the whole thing, but I was so hungry it didn't matter.

While most of us went home during the summer vacation, some students had to stay at school and endure its regime year-round. Betsey Paul remembers:

Us summer boarders had to be working all the time. We picked berries in the hot boiling sun and we weren't allowed to eat any. We were so scared after a little taste of blueberries that we'd go down to the lake and wash our mouths out because if the tell-tale signs were found, we were beaten. Whatever it was—strawberries, raspberries, blueberries, whatever—we always had our mouths checked. "Stick out your tongue," said the nun and if it was red, we lined up for a beating. We were the summer boarders and we didn't go home. It was horrible. We couldn't communicate with anybody.

But then in the wintertime, we'd line up for an egg cup full of cod liver oil followed by an apple. Oh my God, that cod liver oil was awful but it kept us healthy anyway. We became like horses—rugged. But when one got sick, a whole bunch of them got sick and when you were sick, you were punished if you couldn't eat.

Because the children were often too small or too young for the work assigned to them, a number of accidents occurred. One year, the boys were pitching hay in the loft when Maurice Young lost his footing and fell through the opening. He broke his neck and for many months walked around with a neck brace. The girls in the kitchen had to use big machines. Betsey Paul remembers:

There were two pieces of heavy machinery in the kitchen which required a lot of strength to operate. One was the separator for the milk and cream. It consisted of twenty-eight plates which had to be cleaned for the next time around. It took two or three girls to turn the wheel to start it up, but I learned a little short-cut by bracing my foot against the lower part and with all my strength I would pull the handle and the bell would ring. The bell had to ring seven times before you could push the button to start the motor.

The other was the dough mixer. I remember when Georgina Charles caught her hand in the dough mixer. I was working in the refectory when I heard this loud screaming. My God, it was an awful scream—like someone in terrible pain. We all ran down to see what happened and Georgina's hand was all crushed! It was bleeding and everything and it was terrible to see. The poor soul was suffering so much and she was rushed to the hospital. They operated on her hand and she was confined to the infirmary. She had lost the use of her index and third finger but eventually, she regained the partial use of her hand and was able to knit like the rest of us.

I used to work on the dough mixer all the time. I never allowed anyone around it when I was working on it and there was a way to test the dough by taking your foot to get that wheel working to bring the dough up to you instead of putting your hand down in the machine. The bread was baked in an oven which held twenty loaves at a time—ten on the top shelf and ten on the bottom.

The other major task for the girls was working in the laundry, supervised by a nun. The girls did all the washing, drying and ironing for the whole school including sheets, towels, blankets and tablecloths as well as all of the two hundred boys' and girls' clothing. They also washed the ten Sisters' and the priest's everyday clothes, as well as starching the Sisters' collars and caps and ironing the priest's shirts. Every girl who reached grade five was expected to spend her time every year in the laundry. The work was all the harder because the girls were required to wash many of the garments by hand with a washboard rather than using the washer and dryer the school owned. Betsey Paul remembers her time working in the laundry:

It was the same routine year-after-year, day-after-day and if we got caught talking, our heads were bumped together. I was nine years old when they started me off easy, folding clothes in the laundry. At my age, I couldn't even reach the clothesline. Someone had to jump up on the pole and hold the clothesline down so we could hang clothes on it. In a couple of weeks we were doing heavy work. First, we took the dirty clothes and lifted them into the washing machine which was about three feet from the floor. Then when they were washed, we carried them dripping wet to the extractor which spun the water out of them. It was a dangerous machine and if one's hand was caught, it could break.

Some things had to be specially done like the priest's and nun's linen and the Sisters' starched collars and the altar cloth, which was put on rollers so it wouldn't wrinkle.

When I was about ten or eleven years old, I was sent to work in the laundry. My sister Rosie was working on the mangle. At recess time, she came over to where I was working at the washer and warned me about the mangle. The mangle was a red monstrosity of a machine that was about six feet long and about four high with three long rollers that were four inches in diameter—two in the front and one in the back. They rolled around another larger metal roller in the center that was about three feet in diameter. It was heated to a hot enough temperature to dry and iron all the sheets and tablecloths. Two girls stood in the back, one on each end. One girl would take one end of a wet sheet and feed it into the machine, and as it rolled through it was dried and ironed. Two or three girls stood in front of the machine and took the sheet away and folded it. Depending upon whether the sheets were taken off the clothesline or out of the washer, they may have required more than one ironing to dry them. The sheets taken from the extractor were still quite damp and required more than one ironing and because they were wet, they were more apt to get stuck on the rollers and tangle up. Sometimes the sheets were so wet, they had to be taken out and hung on the clothesline no matter how cold it was.

My sister also showed me how to turn the machine off. We were standing near the washer where we could see the bottom of the mangle where there was a two-pronged propeller. She pointed to it and said, "You see that wheel under the mangle? Well, if anybody gets their hands caught in it while you're working there, step on it and the rollers will separate."

Weeks went by. Then one cold afternoon, I heard an inhuman-sounding scream. It went through me like a cold bellowing wind and chilled me right to the core of my bones. I knew immediately what had happened—one of the girls had got her hand caught in the mangle.

A girl in the back of the machine kicked the propeller, but it broke! I watched in horror when I saw her foot kicking at it again and again, trying to make it work, but I could see from where I was standing that it was broken and even when she kicked the other side, nothing happened. The mangle just kept turning, taking Teresa Ginnish's hand with it as it went. Teresa's hand was tangled in the sheets and the sheets were rolling up in the small rollers. Round and round the three rollers went. Farther and farther her little hand went and she was bent over holding onto her elbow with her good hand as if trying to stop it from going in the machine. Her mouth was open and her eyes were filled with tears. Her terrified screams were joined by the screaming and hollering of all the rest of her class which numbered about twenty girls. Some of them were just jumping up and down in one spot—others were running around trying to help each other. Round and round the big steel hot roller rolled. I remember holding my mouth so I wouldn't scream, but my eyes were filling with tears because the two little girls who had been working with her were holding onto her waist as if trying to stop her from being fed into the machine. Rosie was one of them. My sister was yelling and crying too. I was so scared I thought that all the three girls were going to be swallowed up by the mangle.

I could see another girl in the back of the machine jumping up and down trying to reach the switch on the wall behind her to turn the machine off, but it was too high for her. The other girl was lifting her up but she missed. Someone else ran for a chair. In the meantime, out front, the girls were still hanging on to Teresa whose hand kept going in deeper and deeper. We did not know what to do. No one had ever told us what to do in an emergency.

Finally the Sister-in-Charge, Pi'jkwej, came running from the kitchen where she was having a tea break and reached up over the girls' heads and switched off the button. She acted like she saw herself as a heroine.

They pried the sheets off the rollers and released Teresa. A layer of skin from her hand came off with the sheet and she fainted. The girls carried her over to the chair and the nun put a wet cloth over her face and told us to go away. We took a step backward and kept an eye on our little friend. Everyone was crying silently now because she looked so pale and her eyes were rolling up inside her head from side to side with the whites showing and her lips had turned purple. Some other nuns had heard the screaming and had come running from the kitchen and other places. The furnace man and the furnace boys came in from the back and we all stood around not knowing what to do. Finally the nuns sent us to dinner which I don't remember eating and one of the furnace boys carried Teresa away. People said, "They're taking her to the hospital."

When she returned months later, she showed us her hand which was badly scarred. She explained to us that she was in physiotherapy and eventually we saw her regain the use of her fingers. For a couple of weeks after the accident the mangle was not used, until one day we walked in and Pi'jkwej happily announced, "The mangle is fixed."

During the eleven years I was a student at the Residential School, at least four other girls were maimed because they got their hands caught either in the mangle or in the dough mixer in the kitchen. Years later, when researching this book, I came across the official explanation of one of these accidents which Father Mackey had apparently not bothered to report. When the Department of Indian Affairs queried a hospital bill resulting from Christina Nicholas having caught her hand in the mangle, Father Mackey responded that she got caught in the machine because she was trying to warm her hands on the mangle. No one questioned how her hands could be cold working on a steaming machine in a hot laundry. No mention was made of the fact that the emergency switch was too high for the children to reach, or even of the fact that some girls were so small they could not see over the top of the machine, or the fact that the laundry itself was a sweat shop. Most important of all no one questioned leaving twenty girls below the age of sixteen alone to operate heavy machinery. No safety device was ever installed in the eleven years I was there and no safety education was given.

Rigorous standards, however, were required in all our cleaning and polishing tasks. Both boys and girls swept, mopped, waxed and polished all the floors in the school on Saturday morning. The wood floors had to be polished until we could literally see our faces in them. The three flights of stairs on both sides had to be washed every Saturday morning, as did all the cement floors in the lavatories and recreation halls. A few girls suffered from water on the knee as a result of all the kneeling on hard surfaces. Rita Howe remarks of one of her classmates:

> Poor Vernita stayed in bed on the third floor for months with water on the knee. She used to cry all night from the pain and they wouldn't give her anything for it. All they did was change the bandage once a day and raise her leg up on pillows. Finally, it got better by itself, but it took a long time and she missed a lot of school.

Both boys and girls knitted during their spare time which was usually on rainy and stormy days and at playtime. Peter Julian says, "I

These boys are making shoes in the cobbler shop—at front is Bruce Meuse.

still can knit a pair of socks." During World War II we were constantly "knitting for Britain," endlessly making socks, scarves, mittens and sweaters for the military. By the time the war was over both the boys and girls were pretty good knitters. Betsey Paul, like other students, remembers the knitting as enjoyable, "but what really made it so difficult was being told day after day that idleness was the devil's workshop."

Everyone I interviewed liked the sewing Sisters, Clita and Rita because they never yelled or scolded, but taught sewing in a calm and patient way. We all looked forward to Wednesday afternoons because it was two hours away from the oppressive classrooms. Sister Clita was young and pretty, and Sister Rita was a little older and very patient. Both were gentle souls and even allowed us to talk and laugh as long as we were reasonably quiet. The work in the sewing room was difficult because we made all our own clothes from scratch, which involved cutting patterns from heavy rolls of fabric and material. Long tables were lined up like a factory, and girls stood on each side with different-sized patterns which they tried to cut without making a mistake to avoid waste.

Darning everyone's socks was a drag because the holes were so big and so numerous. But I didn't mind it because it was a break away from class and the sewing nuns were nice to work for. Once in a while Wikew took over the sewing class when the other two went on retreats and she'd slap anyone who accidently dropped the burnt-out lightbulbs which were used inside the stocking to hold it in place.

Harriette Battiste who was there in the early thirties said:

> Not all Sisters were bad. Some of them were really nice. They taught us how to tat lace collars which were stylish in those days, crochet doilies and how to decorate our spreads with Mother Goose characters and to sew fancy designs on the altar cloth by using the button hole stitch. One girl, Katie Wilmot, used to make dolls from scratch and dress them up in a full wardrobe right down to the underwear. She was very talented with her hands—nata'-lukwet.

The schedule for the Resi was so heavily geared toward work and prayer that little time was allotted to play. We played for half an hour between the noon meal after the dishes were done at 12:30 and 1:00 when the bell rang for school. We had fifteen minutes for recess in the morning and again at 3:30. After school we had another hour before we would be called in to wash up for supper. There was an hour after supper before Benediction which was taken up in knitting. Total time allowed for play per day was no more than two hours, and sometimes even that was taken from us and we were forced to go on long walks through the village and once, as I recall, to the reserve.

From the time the school opened until the end of World War II the only playground equipment was a baseball diamond with two or three benches around it. Matthew Thomas was a student in 1929 and he told me about a boys' baseball team under Father Pecker, who took over for Father Mackey during one of his illness leaves in 1930:

> Father Pecker picked out the best. We had two teams. The nuns used to get mad because we wouldn't mop the floors because we were out practicing until two o'clock in the afternoon when we'd walk to Shubie and play a game with

Above: Boys in the playground. (The date on the photograph is June 1961). Below: Rod Brown, manual arts teacher, at bat, is teaching the girls how to play baseball while Father Mackey and Indian Agent, H.C. Rice, watch.

the white teams from Stewiacke, Shubie, Milford, and St.
Pat's—we played every doggone team there was. Well, you
take twelve-year-olds who can beat grown men to a score of
twenty to nothing—they must be good. I was the catcher and
I caught everything that was thrown at me. I knew just what
my first base player was going to do. I knew what my pitcher
was going to do. We had everything right down to size. But
when Father Mackey came home we played one game and
beat the daylights out of them, and do you know what he
done? He busted up the team and we never played ball after
that. No way!

I remember my sister Rosie on a ball team. She was good. Not
me—the ball hit my thumb and it swelled up black and blue. My friend
Tiddo pulled it to set it back in place. Crack. Next day it was better
and I was watching the girls playing ball with the boys under the
supervision of Father Mackey.
    "Play ball." My sister was up at bat. Strike one. Oh my God, help.
Strike two. Oh, I can't look. Ball one. Yes, that's it—walk her. Please
walk her. It's better than strike three. The pitcher wound up and threw
the ball and a miracle happened. My prayers were answered. She hit
the ball and started running for first base. SAFE! Thank you God.
Just when I thought it was over, I heard Leona yelling, "Run, Rosie,
run." And Rosie listened to her. She headed for second base and
everyone was trying real hard to get her out. But they couldn't. She
made second base. SAFE! I can't take any more. Another pitch, and
the batter missed. Then everyone yelled, "Run, Rosie, run." Now
what? My sister headed for the third base and was safe again. This
was getting good. I was so excited I chewed my nails so hard they
started bleeding. Leona will get her home, she has everything under
control. She's bossy you know. If she says run, my sister will run.
They're best friends you know—even like the same boys—I heard
them talking. There's another pitch, the batter hit it and Rosie headed
for home. The score keeper put a one beside her name. I saw it! My
big sister is a ball player and she wears a ball cap. They took mine
away from me but I don't care. I hope Rosie doesn't hurt her fingers.
"Rosie, doesn't the ball hurt your fingers?" "No, Leona taught me
how to catch the ball. Her brother Joe taught her last summer when

she went home for vacation."

In the wintertime, when the pond on the boys' side and the marsh on Maitland road froze over, we went skating. The boys skated on their side and we skated on the marsh. Margaret Mary Young and Tiddo were excellent skaters. They both got white skates for Christmas and they used to pair up and skate around the rink—together, backwards, frontwards, in tune and in step. It was an unusual and exciting performance. Every day, they'd entertain us for twenty minutes or so and we'd stand around and watch. We never tired of watching them because they were so good and it was impossible to get jealous of such talent. Both girls were thin and light on their feet and were of a gentle character. They never complained or hurt anyone. They were well liked. When I tried to imitate them, I fell and broke my arm and for a while I went around with a cast.

One afternoon my friend Florence, whom we called Puddenette, and I decided to explore the ice. She called herself Christopher Columbus and me Queen Isabella of Spain and so in order to act like a Queen, I jumped in front of her. The ice gave way and the Queen fell in a dike. It was dry and I found myself eye level to the ground. Between the ground and the ice was a space about one foot deep. Lying there I could see that for miles that space was filled with hanging icicles. It was beautiful and I wanted to crawl in there but I couldn't fit. So instead, Puddenette and I walked in the dike all afternoon, admiring the scenery. This was our secret but not for long. About the same time, we had learned a new word, catastrophe. That afternoon, everything was a catastrophe. At the supper table, Puddenette was telling everybody about the icicles and saying, "What a catastrophe!" And all the kids would say, "Ooh" and "Aah" because they knew it was pretty—like a chandelier.

During the wintertime, we'd build snowhouses and snowforts and have snowball fights. Wikew would look out from the third storey windows and look inside our snowhouses and watch what we were doing because they had no roofs. Kids would warn each other, "Wikew is looking out the window." I remember seeing the girls' yard filled with about ten snowmen. Some wore hats and scarves and mittens and had coals for eyes and stick noses and mouths. The yard was alive. At night, before we went to bed, we'd stand by the window and say goodnight to them. They looked alive in the moonlight with the stars sparkling overhead and crispy snow sparkling in all the surrounding fields. The snowmen were all different sizes because the bigger girls were able to lift their snowballs higher than the little girls could but then they would help each other. Some had made snowsteps in order to reach the head and put on the face. The snowmen were facing in every direction. Some faced the school, and some faced the town. A couple faced the open fields out back. For days after school, the girls left little presents in the holes at the foot of their snowmen. These presents included beads, necklaces, rings, bobby pins, bows made from yarn, and buttons, which were a popular item, especially if they came from a boy's shirt found in the laundry, and notes written in code which we thought the nuns would never decipher. The code was 1=a, 2=b, 3=c and so on. Other times, we'd make snowdragons, and snowhorses and a big pile of snowballs. Then we'd have snowball fights and smash them down.

We made rings for our fingers from the rings that come with sink and tub stoppers which we filed down on the cement floor in the recreation hall. Neat necklaces were made by stringing two of the chains together. But you couldn't let Wikew see it, unless of course you had a holy medal of Our Lady of Perpetual Help, or The Sacred Heart or St. Theresa the Little Flower attached to it. There was some red and pink crepe paper in the top presses that was stored away for the banners used in the May Procession and other church events like First Communion and Confirmation. Just spit on it and rub it on your lips, cheeks, fingernails and toenails for lipstick, rouge and nail polish. In the summertime, just top it off with a necklace, crown and wrist band made from dandelions. You can always chew on the stems if you get hungry. One time a girl dangled a string of six or seven safety pins from her blouse pocket and Wikew got mad and called her a dirty girl because the safety pins were used to pin our pads onto our belts during our menses.

Rita Howe remembers coming across a treasure trove:

> When we were cleaning out the presses, and when Aniap turned her back, we looked inside the boxes that were kept there and that's when we found all that fancy lingerie. There were silk slips, bras, panties and nightgowns—all colours, white, black, pink. Holy cow! I wonder who these belong to.

I bet they belong to the nuns when they went on vacation. I even held them up to myself and admired how pretty they looked. I thought about Mamma right away. I bet she'd like this. She never had a silk nightgown or slip in her life. My friends and I tucked as many as we could inside our bloomer legs and buried them in a hole we dug out behind the clotheslines for safekeeping until June when we will be going home for the summer. We used to count the sleeps before going home— three more sleeps, then two and finally only one. On that last day, we ran out behind the clothesline and dug up the fancy lingerie. When we lifted them up to examine them, they were all in shreds. What a disappointment that was. We hadn't thought of wrapping them up to protect them from rotting.

Sometimes our fantasies were based on the few movies we'd seen—mostly cowboy films where the Indians got slaughtered. One year I came back from vacation and a group of us girls were gathered around the swings just as it was getting dark, all talking excitedly about what kind of summer we'd had, when one of them suggested we act out a Roy Rogers movie the summer girls had seen. "I'm Roy and you're Dale," she said. Then we went galloping on our make-believe horses and she began strumming her imaginary guitar and singing a cowboy song—"Happy Trails to You." Then she and I galloped off into the sunset, and after we got a little ways, she stopped me with a movie-style embrace and stuck her tongue in my mouth and said, "The End."

Sometimes we would scratch our fantasies of "dream houses" in the dirt of the playground. I remember pacing off a house on the ground. It was about ten paces wide and twelve paces long. There was a front door and a back door and windows in every room. Usually it was a two-storey house with bedrooms and the bathroom upstairs. The windows had lace curtains and the floors were covered with rugs with floral designs. Fancy dishes were drawn on the dining room table and a tea set sat on a buffet. Lacy spreads and pillowcases covered the beds. Our dream houses were designed in imitation of the priest's suite and the nuns' rooms. Some girls were very artistic and imaginative and for a while got lost in a world of electricians, interior decorators, architects and builders. They would furnish each room with over-

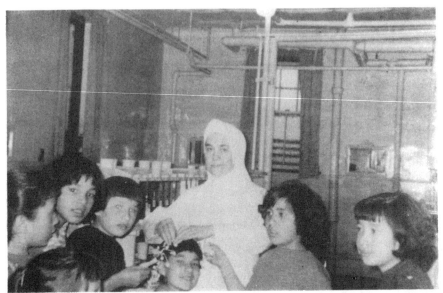

After Father Collins took over in 1958, the atmosphere at the school was more relaxed. The girls were even allowed to have their hair permed.

stuffed couches and armchairs, and radios, all drawn right down to the last details on the rugs, mats, curtains and spreads. They drew elaborate accessories such as crystal chandeliers and chinaware, silverware, butter dishes, creamers and sugarbowls by using bobby pins and safety pins. Our blue-print homes were surrounded by hedges, a lawn, trees, bird houses, a garden and even a fountain. Then the rain would come and wash the house drawing away and we'd start all over again with a new house in a new location and maybe with a new family.

One afternoon, Wikew called us in from the yard and announced that we were going for a walk. We lined up with a partner and set off for the reserve road but this time instead of turning off at the checkerboard sign, we kept going right up to the reserve, right to the meadows where I lived. My father was sitting in his undershirt hewing out axe handles. He stood up when he saw us and shook Wikew's hand—so polite. My Mom came out of the kitchen in her apron and gave the nun some corn from the garden. It was quite high and ripe. This was an unexpected treat for Rosie and me since we got to see our parents and our home, but it was spoiled by feeling everyone else watching us. Later on, somebody told me we were poor. I never knew that. I never felt poor in my whole life until one of the summer girls who never went home told me, "You're poor." And I didn't reply because from the tone of her voice I thought it was a shameful thing to be.

Playtime was hard to distinguish from worktime because it was often interrupted by special chores that had to be done. Sometimes it only consisted of long walks through the village of Shubenacadie, often in intense cold and with full bladders. The school was situated on a hill with no trees to provide shelter. The girls' side faced northwest while the boys' side, southeast. The winds came from all directions, swirled around the building and up the sides, so on either side you could get caught in a whirlwind. In the wintertime, the children tried to find shelter from the biting cold by huddling together in the corner, from which they were chased away by the nuns. Peter Julian says:

> We used to take the little boys and put them in the middle and we'd all huddle in the corner to get some relief from the cold. Their hands and feet would be cold and they'd be shivering. Then Chico would come along and chase us away from the corner.

On the girls' side, we got the full impact of the north wind. The girls wore woolen skirts which looked warm but the wind blew up them and chilled the whole body from the spine up. We'd be standing there jumping up and down so our feet would not freeze because we wore rubber boots which are meant to keep the wet out but which draw the cold. Kids used to chew on their mittens because they were hungry and the mittens would freeze. Their noses would run and that would freeze. We'd huddle in the corner like cattle each trying to get a little warmth from the other body. Rosie used to come over and wrap her coat around me until she got cold then she'd go right back out in the yard and run around to get warm again while I stood there and cried. She used to tell me. "If you keep moving, you won't get so cold." Then Wikew would open the window or door and yell, "Get away from that corner and go play." And we'd all walk away with our heads bent down into the freezing cold. Little girls were so cold they could barely walk. Sometimes they'd lose bladder control so they got a beating on the cold legs when they got inside. "Lift up your skirt," the nun would holler. Then she would beat them with a long-handled shoehorn which she affectionately called her "shillelagh."

I remember Wikew hitting a little girl with that shoehorn. Her hands were all red and swollen from the cold. The girl put her little hand up to protect herself and Wikew hit it. Then she put her other hand over it and Wikew hit that one. I could see her suppressing her cries of pain and bending her knees to brace herself against another attack. Then when it came, there was just a silent whimper because the child was too terrified to cry out. Someone told me the first whack warmed the hands and you didn't feel the rest.

But on the good days, the coasting on the hill was fabulous. The double runners, which sat six to nine kids, were made by a blacksmith who joined two sleds together with boards. One day I fell off one and suffered a swollen and bruised face and neck when it rolled right over my head. As luck would have it, the two-hundred-pound Wikew was a passenger that day. But I was saved from serious injury by the heavy scarf and hat I wore.

One winter a girl who was about nine fell off a double runner and broke her leg. Wikew told her to stand up. Irene was crying and saying, "It hurts, my leg is broken." But Wikew said, "If you can stand on it, it's not broken, so stand on it." She ordered two girls to take her, an arm on each side, and make her walk. They did as they were told while the rest of us watched in fear for we could see that she was in great pain. When she sat back down and took off her stocking, her knee was swollen bigger than two and it was turning blue so Wikew said, "Take her to the nurse." And the three girls went hobbling away to the refectory where the first aid station was located.

Some parents sent skis to their children at Christmas time, but the rest of us had to improvise by making skis out of barrel staves from the old apple barrels dumped behind the kitchen. We rubbed them over the cement floor to make them smooth, then waxed and polished them. Then we'd go flying down over that hill all day long. The boys were doing the same thing on the other side or out back behind the furnace.

With signs of spring in the air, we'd begin making skipping ropes. Rolls of paper fibre strands were brought down to the recreation hall and cut in lengths about twelve to sixteen feet long. Any longer and they'd be too heavy after they were braided. One girl would tie a knot using three ends and hold the end while three other girls took one strand each and stood on the other end. Then they would weave the rope. The girl on the end on the right would walk under the arm of the girl in the middle and take her rope over the head of the girl on the left. Then the process was repeated over and over until the whole thing was braided. Even the girls' footsteps made rhythmic shuffling sounds on the floor which made it a dance. Throughout the recreation hall, other braids of different sizes were being made and the air was filled with anticipation and excitement.

When the playgrounds became dry enough, the skipping season began for both girls and boys. Other spring and summer games were basketball, marbles and of course hopscotch. On rainy days, there were table-top games such as checkers with a homemade checker-board and homemade cardboard checkers, and playing cards from homemade cardboard decks painted with crayons.

I remember going to Skite'kmuj's class and her saying, "Put your books away because today we are going to have fun. We are going to tell stories and sing songs. Does anybody know a song they want to sing?" Peter Joseph raised his hand and volunteered to sing it for the class. He went up front and started to sing: "They left the pig in the parlour, they left the pig in the parlour, they left the pig in the parlour the night before the storm." This was sung to the tune of, "The Bear went over the Mountain." Everybody started laughing and Peter Joseph was enjoying his ability as an entertainer. I was sitting in the front row and I was getting a good chuckle out of the song when I saw her coming towards him. I didn't realize what she was going to do because she had told us this was going to be fun-time and I believed her. Skite'kmuj was as white as the ghost she was named after and she had the pointer in her hand. Peter Joseph's back was facing her so she caught him unaware and vulnerable. She came down on his collarbone with the pointer with such force that he almost collapsed. By the time the pointer hit his shoulder, it was too late to warn him. She began yelling, "You dirty, dirty boy. You look like you would leave a pig in the parlour, doesn't he class?" Gee, he looked nice and clean to me. His shirt was always neat and his hair was always combed down—not sticking up like mine. And he had a neat sense of humour too.

For a brief time we had some enjoyable "Physical Training" lessons. One of the younger Sisters gave us mats and taught us "the bicycle." While she was demonstrating this, revealing her long navy blue bloomers, Wikew walked in. After two or three sessions the Physical Training classes came to an abrupt end. The rumour circulated that Wikew had put a stop to it because she was jealous.

We were never allowed to own anything personal. Shirley Stephens who was a pupil during Father Collins' time told me:

> One day I was digging in the yard and I found an old coin. I showed it to Father Collins and he offered me fifty cents for it. I refused. Later that day I was in the lavatory washing the dirt off the coin and Sister came in from behind me and asked me nicely to give her the coin and I said, "No Sister, I want to keep it because I think it's an antique." I was hanging onto it real tight because it was mine. I found it. But Sister pried it from my fingers and took it. She told me in a nice way, "I'll keep it in a safe place for you and when you go home, you can have it back." But I never saw the coin again.

When I think about the games we played and the things we did to entertain ourselves it seems that whatever was happening Wikew would find a way to spoil it. She would find some little girl to beat up or insult or make fun of, or poke in the ribs with her finger or pull her hair or say, "What are you grinning at?" or, "Wipe that smile off your face," or, "Put your crocodile tears in your pocket," after she had given a vicious beating. It was not unusual for her to come running into the recreation hall with her face red with anger swinging a skipping rope or whatever she could grab and yell, "Get out you little savages (or wild Indians, or heathens)."

For me, relief from all this came every Sunday when Mom and Dad came to see us and brought food—mostly home-made blueberry pies and we'd get to be a family for an hour. Afterwards, when she saw blueberry stains on our teeth Wikew would say in her usual sarcastic way. "Isabelle and Rosie had blueberry pie in the parlour." But I didn't care because I was enjoying the blueberries we had picked during the summer to eat in the winter. Sometimes we had apple pie from apples our parents picked in the fall and dried for winter food.

It was good to be with my three brothers and to see they still had their hair. If any one of us had a bad week, Mom would hug and hold us and rock us gently in the rocking chair in the parlour with our heads in her lap because we were getting pretty big now to sit in her lap. Sometimes Rosie and I sang hymns that we learned in the choir and performed religious plays from Sunday school while Joe acted the producer and stage hand. One time they brought licorice pipes and we sat around imitating the elders smoking and talking and saying, "A'a." My parents laughed so hard and gave us names. Henry pretended he was Chief, and Joe imitated Uncle Ben while Noel talked like Uncle Martin. Rosie and I impersonated Mrs. Gloade and Aunt Sabet. Then in no time at all the joking had to end and I had to part from them and find a way to face the long week ahead.

I took this picture of the room we called "The Dungeon" when I visited the derelict school. It was one of the windowless soap closets where runaway boys were locked, sometimes for several days and nights. They would be strapped and their heads shaved bald in front of all the kids. The nun would bring them out at mealtimes, when they were given only dry bread and water. After we said Grace at the end of the meal, the nun would lock them in the room again and replace the skeleton key in her pocket.

 CHAPTER 4

REWARDS AND PUNISHMENTS

I remember those horrifying years as if it were yesterday. There was one nun, Sister Gilberta, she always passed out the punishment. Every day, she would take me into the bathroom and lock the door. She would then proceed to beat me thirty times on each hand, three times a day, with a strap. She would count to thirty, out loud, each time she hit me. It's an awful way to learn to count to thirty. My older sister, Grace, learned to count to fifty.

I never understood why I had to get those beatings, but at the age of 37, I realize it had to be because I spoke my language. To this day, I can't speak my language very well. But I do understand when I am spoken to in Micmac.

Why was our culture and language such a threat that it had to be taken away from us with such vengeance?

To be taught your language with respect and kindness by your people, then to have the White Man pull it from your heart with meanness and torture. Some people wonder why we are so tough, because we had to be, we had no choice.

I have polio and it affected my bladder and as a child, I wet my pants a lot. I received extra beatings for that too.

Once I was thrown across the dorm floor by Sister Gilberta. At the age of six, it seemed far away. I bounced off the wall at the other end of the dorm. I was sore on one side of my body for a few days.

—Imelda Brooks, Big Cove, N.B.
Micmac-Maliseet News
May 1991

I don't remember ever receiving any rewards from any nun for anything I have ever done except for the laundry. I helped in the laundry and the nun there was very good to me and every morning she would give me one piece of candy or chocolate. She just did it I think from the goodness of her heart and I always did my work whether I received a reward or not. I think the Sister was trying to get a good relationship based on good terms—love, respect and admiration which I gave her. When I went to visit her, she was eighty years old exactly and she was so glad to see me and she just cried and held out her arms and I went into them and we hugged each other and our tears mingled. I went to visit that Sister because of that friendship established many years ago.

I saw the favorites and pets get rewards of ribbon, candy, bread and jam, medals and holy cards. And to children who never received presents at Christmas time those things meant a lot. One thing I can say about the Sister on the girls' side is that she let me have skates when I was fifteen, one year away from going home for good. During summer vacations, she tried not to be as mean as during the school year. She held back her anger and didn't scold as much. She let us get away with little things like sleeping in. They took us to Grand Lake once. We had to pick blueberries. When we had a bowl full of berries, she rewarded us with candy—a B.B. sucker—one candy—a B.B.sucker. I have to think really hard to remember the rewards.

—Rita Joe
Mi'kmaw poet

Rather than trying to inspire us to be creative or to motivate us to do well, the teachers at the school relied on orders, threats and ridicule. They had no interest, apparently, in anything we might have thought or felt. Such rewards as were meted out depended on the nuns' whims. Even if you won something by chance it could be snatched away from you. I remember there was a bingo for someone's left-over Christmas present and we all sat around to try to win a surprise that Wikew had. I didn't really care what it was as long as I won it. I was set for B-15, but she called B-14 and I got so excited I went, "Whew! That was close." and I blew all the pieces of paper I was using for markers off the card. Everyone sitting at my table started to help me get them back on when an older girl reminded us, "You don't have to do that, just wait for one number." Just then we heard B-15 called. Everyone started yelling, "Bingo, Isabelle got Bingo!" Wikew took out a white fur hat and said, "Here is your prize. Come over and try it on." I walked over and she put it on my head and tied the furry tassels under my chin. "Turn around and let me see what you look like." Then she made a funny face and said, "This hat does not look nice on you. Girls, do you think this hat looks good on Isabelle?" And all the little girls looked at me, then at her, with a puzzled look but didn't say anything. "No," she continued the conversation with herself, "she does not look nice at all. Isabelle, do you want to wear a hat that does not look nice on you?"

"No Sister." I didn't really care what it looked like. All I knew was that it felt nice and warm and furry.

"Okay, take it off. Margaret come over and try on this hat. I think it will look nice on you."

As a child, I lived in perpetual fear of saying and doing anything, even if it was good, for if my work was too good, I knew that it would bring the response, "Who do you think you are? You think you're such a big shot!" And I was always afraid to do my best. If I knew my work was good, I made sure that I didn't finish it. Then, the nun could only yell, "Why didn't you finish the job I asked you to do?" To me, that was better than being ridiculed. I remember the incident that taught me this. We were given the task of embroidering the altar cloth with fine designs of grapes, roses, and flowers, and with little crosses along the edges. Pauline Johnson was very artistic and adept with her hands and her work was excellent. Sewing was no effort for her and she would chat and sew merrily along while the rest of us struggled with threading fine needles and got all tangled up. In no time, she had a whole section finished. Wikew came down from her prayers and examined our work. When she saw what Pauline had done, she was furious and instead of being pleased and praising her she began yelling, "Who told you to continue sewing? You did not have my permis-

sion to sew this much, so rip it all up again and we'll see who the
smart one around here is. You sit there looking so proud of yourself.
You look as proud as Lucifer. Say it, I'm proud as Lucifer."

Pauline mumbled, "I'm proud as Lucifer."

Wikew, "Say it louder so everyone can hear you. Here, stand on
the bench and say it so the girls in the back of the room can hear you."

There always seemed to be something arbitrary about the way any
treats were handed out. I remember Wikew walking into the recreation
hall with a bowl of candy or peanuts and throwing handfuls of goodies
on the floor while she stood and watched us scramble for them. I was
never good at scrambling. She always came in unexpectedly while we
were busy knitting or playing. Other times, she'd walk in the hall with
a plate piled high with toast covered with jam which was left over
from the Sisters' dining room. We would stand around looking at the
plate, hoping to get a slice. She would call each girl by name and
they'd step up one by one and walk away with their bread while the
rest of us waited for our turn which sometimes did not come.

There was no recognition for service, for achievement or for work
completed or well done. We received no certificates, diplomas, or
awards for school grades, promotions, arts or sports. The only real
recognition was to crown the statue of the Virgin Mary during the
annual May Procession, or to read the accompanying prayer, or to sing
solo at Midnight Mass.

Once the girls' choir won the prize as the best choir in Hants
County schools and was invited to sing on CBC Halifax's program,
"Fireside Frolics." The trophy was presented to Sister Gilberta and
displayed in a glass case in the front hall leading to the chapel for one
year. It was only on loan and, after the year was up, had to be returned
to the school board. Russell Brooks, who was a student after the war,
recalls seeing a scroll that held all the names of former students who
had served in the military and been killed during World War II. For a
long time it hung on the wall leading to the chapel but when the school
closed down, the scroll was never found.

I remember singing solo one Christmas Eve, "Oh Holy Night" and
"Adeste Fidelis." That afternoon, I developed a cold and had to suck
on a lemon and go to bed early. At eleven they woke me up, gave me
some cocoa and I sang like an angel. Mommie and Daddy were in the
audience as well as several other people from the Reserve. Frankly, I

These girls are dressed up for the May Procession: Margaret Julian, Mary Anne Battiste, Marie Pictou, Teresa Joe, unknown.

was not the best singer they could have chosen. Most of the choir girls had better singing voices and a better sense of rhythm than I, although I do have a good ear and I know a good singer when I hear one. I often wondered why Leona Copage wasn't picked. After a while it dawned on me that favouritism had more to do with the selection of soloists than singing ability. The fact that my parents were regular visitors at the school not only saved me from many punishments but also meant I was sometimes singled out for preferential treatment. However, I was never picked for the supreme honour of crowning Mary. One year this was decided by election and Nora Bernard remembers being voted by her peers as the one to do the honours:

> It was my last year there and we had elections and I was voted as the favourite. Sister Mary Charles did not take the news too well and called me into her office and told me why I should give my votes to Lillian so she'd have something to

remember the school by . . . So instead of being given the
honour I was due, I was allowed to read the valedictory
which meant nothing to me. I was so jealous I was wishing
the statue would topple over, or that Lillian would slip or
something.

If the rewards were meagre and slow in coming, the punishments
were plentiful and swift. By the early 1950s the school's reputation
had spread throughout the Native community, so that on many reserves, "Don't do that or you'll be sent to Shubie," was a standard
threat to children. The school was so strongly associated with punishment in children's minds that those who were "sent to Shubie" as a
result of their family circumstances constantly wondered what crime
they had committed. For many of them the school's reputation as a
place of punishment proved all too accurate.

Throughout both Father Mackey's and Father Collins' regimes the
biggest crime was running away. Runaways were brought back in a
cop car by the RCMP. Their heads were shaved and they were kept in
the dark broom and soap closet, sometimes for several days and
nights. They were strapped and fed only dry bread and water. In one
case, the boys were tied to a chair and left there for two days. Matthew
Thomas and his wife Katie Copage were both students in 1934 when
Bruce Labrador and Joe Toney ran away and were brought back. They
told me that the two boys had their heads shaved and had their hands
tied behind their backs. They were strapped to a chair with a Bible on
their laps which they were supposed to read. They had to sit in the
broom closet all day and all night and all the next day without permis-
sion to go to the bathroom. These were Father Mackey's orders. Then
they ran away again and were brought back and the same thing happened.

Peter Julian recalls the treatment given to runaways:

When I first landed there, I think it was the first time that I
ever seen my brother Joe and I heard that he ran away. He
was picked up by the RCMP and brought back. Sister Paul of
the Cross stripped him down to the waist and shaved off all
his hair. Bald! I was just a young boy and I pitied my brother
but I didn't dare cry. They had a closet which they called the

dark hole that had no windows and it was located just underneath the steps where they locked runaways and bad kids and
the only time they saw any light was when their meals of dry
bread and water were served them. They were taken from
there and up to Mackey and given the same type of beating
I got. I don't know how long they were put on this bread and
water, sometimes maybe a week and very light food after.
There were quite a few boys who ran away and every one of
them got the same treatment when they returned.

The Sister had the same kind of strap as Father Mackey's.
I remember Peter Michael Stevens was acting the fool one
evening in the dormitory and when he was told to keep quiet
he kept it up so he was told to pull his pants and underwear
down and lay across his bed. Sister Paul of the Cross put a
strapping across his bum and after the first blow he rolled
right over on his back with his front showing. But Sister
didn't stop at that. She laced it right across his privates and
the poor boy let out a scream that could be heard all over the
dormitory and Sister hollered, "The longer you lay that way,
the longer I'm going to keep whacking." So he rolled back
again. She was a sadist.

On numerous occasions children were punished despite being
seriously ill. Betsey Paul remembers:

I used to sit at the same table with Dorothy Doucette. She
was so sick, she used to puke right in her plate and Wikew
used to beat her in the mouth with a spoon and stuff the food
mixed with vomit right back into her mouth again. While she
was pinching her cheeks, Sister Paul of the Cross, said,
"This girl is sick, get her to a doctor." Wikew answered,
"Mind your own business Sister. You look after the boys and
I'll take care of the girls." So Sister Paul went and reported
it to Sister Superior who came through the scullery door in
the back and caught her in the act. Wikew was dumbfounded.
It was learned that this was going on for a week and that
Dorothy was losing weight. Sister Superior called Dr. McInnes
and Dorothy was quarantined on the third floor in the infir-

mary because she had been diagnosed as having diphtheria.

Many of the punishments were meted out almost absent-mindedly. I remember during the late thirties coming across a little girl huddled in the dark corner under the stairway in the evening. She told me that she had been there all day, "Will you tell Sister that I'm still here? I've been sitting here all day since this morning." When I told Wikew she said, "Oh my goodness, I forgot all about her. Tell her she can go to bed now."

Father Mackey introduced boxing for the boys more for its value as a means of intimidation than as a form of recreation. Forced boxing matches were a way of keeping the boys in line. Doug Knockwood remembers:

> Gordon Tuplin from Prince Edward Island was the number one fighter and champion boxer and when Andrew Julian from Indian Brook had a disagreement with Gordon at play he was made to go in the squared circle with him. After six rounds, when Father Mackey saw that Andrew was winning, he put on Gordon's gloves and stepped into the ring against Andrew. Because of that religious trip, Andrew wouldn't throw a punch. He just tried to protect himself and finally, he broke down and cried. That was the end of the fight. Father Mackey used his position in the church to intimidate because he knew that Indian children were taught that a priest was a holy man and was doing God's work and he was always right, therefore no one should hit a priest. Father Mackey used strappings and boxing to demonstrate his power over all the boys in front of the entire school.

Isaac Knockwood and Angus Cope, who were students during the forties, were called into Father Mackey's office for a minor offence and the priest hit fifteen-year-old Angus unexpectedly in the jaw so hard it lifted him right off the floor and knocked him out. Then he hit Isaac, who was the same age, with such force it made his head spin.

Some boys began to develop the notion during World War II that Father Mackey might even be in league with the Nazis. Andrew Julian became convinced that Father Mackey was "part German" and he recalls: "During the war, we listened to the German news by Gabriel Heeter on the square radio hanging from the ceiling in the recreation hall. When France was freed, we didn't listen. But we listened to the Max Schmelling and Joe Louis championship fight. When Max Schmelling won by a knockout . . . Father Mackey was step-dancing on the boys' side. He was a good dancer. Sister Adrian served him tea and sandwiches which he ate in front of the boys." Although there seems to be no evidence that Father Mackey was "part-German," it is not so surprising that the young Mi'kmaw boys would develop that belief at the sight of the priest dancing with glee at the defeat of a famous Black boxer.

Peter Julian was another of the unfortunate students in the dilemma of facing in the boxing ring the priest he had been taught to respect:

> I found the punishments extremely severe. I got punishments and I got beatings. One day I got into a fight with another boy and Father Mackey put boxing gloves on the both of us and when I won Father Mackey told me. "You think you're tough." and I said, "No, I don't think I'm tough." I was fourteen years old at the time. Then he put on a pair of boxing gloves and I had no choice. It was either that or a strapping. He had the boys put benches around to represent the ring. He was a big man and I was only a small boy for my age. Besides I had respect for him and wouldn't hit him, but he made me angry and I hit him. Then he got mad and knocked me right over the benches and up against the pillar . . . It dazed me a little bit but it didn't knock me out. Then I told the priest, "I've had enough." But he forced me to get back in the ring and again I felt that I had no choice. I went this far with him and ended up with a lucky punch and hit him in the face. He then ordered the fight stopped and took off his boxing gloves. "Come with me," he said and we went up to his parlour, "and we'll find out how tough you really are. Unbuckle your belt and drop your pants and underpants." I did what he told me to do and then he ordered, "Grasp your ankles." After which he warned me, "You're going to get ten straps right across your bum." He had a strap

about three or four inches wide. He wrapped that around his
hand a couple of times and asked me to bend over. I bent
over and that's when I got it, eh? I spent about three days
nursing my ass because it was so sore and I had a lot of
bruises. I received many serious beatings after that because
if I did something wrong I was sent directly to Father Mackey.

Being hit in the face with the priest's fist was not reserved for
punishing boys, as Rita Howe recalls:

I was at the school in 1949 when Father Mackey was Principal. Barbara Paul was not liked by the Sisters and she was
severely punished for saying the word "sow." It was just
slang to her and she really didn't mean anything or point to
any particular person when she said it that day. We were
washing the walls in the hallway and Barbara was standing
on a ladder reaching high when her wash rag fell out of her
hands. She said, "Oh sow." and Sister heard her and told her
not to repeat it again. The following day Father Mackey
came into the classroom looking for Barbara and when she
went to the front of the class, he asked her if she had said the
word "sow," and she answered, "Yes." She explained that it
was an accident and that she was sorry and promised not to
say it again. Then he hauled off and smashed her in the face,
not with an open hand, but with a fist. She fell down and he
told her to get up. She got up again and he smashed her again
with both fists this time. She went down again and he ordered her up again. He even pushed some of the desks back
to get at her. I think she tried to crawl away, but her nose and
mouth were bleeding and he smashed her again and she went
down again but didn't get up. She tried to sit up half way. He
looked at her and walked out. And it frightened every kid in
the school. I was looking at the windows and thinking about
jumping out to get away. The classroom was grade five and
every kid was screaming and crying while the Sister just
stood there with her arms folded. She didn't do anything. I
swear to God, she enjoyed it. Afterward, the Sister took
Barbara out. I don't know where she took her but the rest of

the day, she wasn't in class.

I can see that chubby fist of Father Mackey's yet. His hands were fat. They looked like they had a ball of fat on top of them.

Because punishment was often meted out based on hearsay evidence, "ratting" on other students, particularly on the boy's side, became a way of working off old scores. One student in the late 1950s recalls that someone telling the nun in charge that you'd been heard speaking Mi'kmaw was a way to ensure that "you'd get the shit beat out of you." Older boys would also intimidate younger ones, "You had to pay for protection. You had to watch your bed—they'd piss in your bed to get you in trouble. In the morning you'd get the blame and you'd have to wear the sheet on your head and parade around." Another cruel trick which some of the boys would play was to loosen the top of the salt shaker so that the next boy who tried to salt his food would have it covered in salt. Not only was his food spoiled, but everyone knew that the nun would force him to eat the whole plateful even if he gagged or vomited.

Many students remember the systematic humiliations which they suffered at least as vividly as the physical pain. More than three decades after the school's closing many students still feel a sense of violation and shame. One woman recalls that some forms of humiliation were worse than the physical pain of beatings:

One day, the girls were climbing on the door onto the roof and sliding down the wall and I followed them. We were playing Follow the Leader. When I was halfway up, the nun caught me. I was afraid of heights but I was even more afraid of what was going to happen to me when I came down— what the nun was going to do. The Sister had a bat. I saw the bat in her hands. When I was hanging onto the door she hit me on the bottom with the bat and I fell to the ground. She hit me again on the arm. The pain was so bad but I didn't cry. She hit me more than once. I was gritting my teeth fighting back the crying but my tears were flowing. It was fear.

The most degrading experience in my life was when the Sister in charge of the girls lined us up and made us hold our panties in our hands for examination. We used to wash the stains quickly and wear our underwear wet. We didn't know why we were afraid. We were afraid of the unknown. Everything to them was a sin.

Nora Bernard recalls that same humiliating inspection of underwear:

I don't know what Sister Wejipsetamite'w's [the sniffer] problem was, for instance, she used to have us girls form a line and take the crotch of our panties and spread them on the palm of our hands as we all walked by her so she could see if they were dirty. She told us that she didn't want us going to church smelly but why didn't she have all of us take a bath or shower before church?

Rita Howe remembers that the nightly sense of dread as she awaited the inevitable humiliation:

I just dreaded going to bed because I knew she was going to do that. When we got ready for bed, Wejipsetamite'w would be watching us. Certain time to get our nightdresses on and certain time to get into bed. While the kids were crawling into bed, she'd watch who was taking their underwear off then she'd go and peek inside of them. We had to take our panties and place them over our clothes at the foot of the bed. Wejipsetamite'w would come to the bottom of the bed and she'd take our underwear and she'd look inside of it then she'd put it back down. She'd go to the next bed, open up the bloomers and do that about twenty-six times which was the number of girls in that dorm. I'd be lying in bed so embarrassed, watching her coming closer and waiting till she got to my bed. It was so humiliating that she was invading my privacy. It seemed that we were being punished for something that was never explained. . . . I don't know if she got a kick from looking at all the girl's underwear or was this to embarrass or degrade or make us ashamed.

During the 1950s the nun in charge of the girls' side decided that the girls would no longer be provided with sanitary towels at night. Only those with exceptionably light periods were able to avoid bleeding onto the sheets. Every morning the sheets had to be held up for inspection. Some girls remember being sent to wash out the bloodstains. Others were beaten as well. For some girls, being beaten four days out of every month became a routine event.

Many of the punishments had a sexual character or association. One former student remembers all the boys being treated for something, perhaps scabies, that "was going around." "They got some white medicine in a bottle that they used to spread on our genitals. They would line us up in the bathroom. We could have put it on for ourselves, but they preferred to do it. You've got boys nine, ten, eleven—some of them would get erections and then the nuns would get mad and beat them." Another student recalls being beaten because he resisted sexual interference. Apparently he was ill and had blacked out in church. He woke up back in the dormitory: "A nun was sponge bathing me and she proceeded to go a little too far with her sponge bathing. So I pushed her hand away. She held my legs apart while she strapped the inside of my thighs. I never stopped her again." The same student recalls that other students taught him a form of meditation technique so that he was able to mentally remove himself from what was happening to his body.

> Some of the other kids told me the secret of how to deal with that was to run away to the pipes. When we finished showering—they'd powder you—and sometimes they'd powder your genitals a little too long . . . One of the kids that was with me used to tell me, "Run away to the pipes." In the shower room there used to be pipes and he told me to pretend that I'm up there on that pipe. Really think about it. You're crawling down to the end—and then there's dust—and then you meet the joint—the elbow—one pipe would be too hot— so you don't go down there—you go down the other one. By the time you're finished travelling the pipes—usually the act is over. That's how I learned to cope with it—by running away to the pipes . . .

Offering more definite resistance was riskier. One student recalls a priest or a brother invoking religion to try to persuade him to perform oral sex.

> I was only a nine-year-old kid. I don't know whether he was a priest or a brother. He had on a black gown—that outfit that they wear. He told me that he works for God, that God is his friend, and if I did things for him then God would take me to heaven. I remember he opened a drawer—he was standing next to his desk—and he opened a drawer and put his leg up there. He had nothing on underneath—I could see his face—his hairy legs . . . I wouldn't—so he strapped me and told me that I was going to Hell.

Most of those who were students at the school have exceptionally vivid memories of the instruments of punishment, as well as the particular incidents when they were used. Nora Bernard describes the main instrument of punishment during the forties as "a strap made out of leather which was about two or three inches wide and a little over two feet long." Yvette Toney, who was a pupil in the late fifties, remembers that the strap during those years was a piece cut out from the rubber mat on the floor leading to the back door. It was about four inches wide and eighteen inches long. The noticeable gap in the mat served as a constant reminder every time children went out and came in from play of the potential punishment that constantly awaited them.

Other straps made of different materials seem to have been in use earlier on. One man recalls:

> I was ordered to polish floors and Sister Superior opened the closet where the polisher was kept. The strap was hanging on a hook behind the door. I touched it and it had a good grip—a wooden handle. It was about four inches wide and about sixteen inches long and a little thicker than my belt and it was cut into strips. It looked like a piece from a conveyor belt from a lumber mill and it was used by Mr. McLeod [the school handyman] and Father Mackey when they lashed the boys.

Another man recalls being ordered to destroy one of the straps immediately before a visit from the school inspectors:

> I was a furnace-hand and Sister Superior came down with a brown paper bag tucked under her cape. She told me that the inspectors came from Ottawa and would I please burn this paper bag and its contents. When I took the bag from her, she turned around right quick and started going up the stairs leading to the laundry. Then she stopped and looked at me and said, "Don't look in the bag, just burn it." As soon as she got out of sight, I peeked in the bag and there were three whips in it. They were cut into strips with a knot tied at the ends—the kind you can send away for in a farmer's catalogue.

In the classroom, the ever-present instrument of punishment was the pointer. Every time the Sister came beside me, I ducked, because I was afraid she was going to hit me with the pointer. Nancy Marble, who became a student a year after the school was founded, was hit on the head with the pointer so frequently that by the time she was fourteen she had lost her hearing. Betsey Paul's memories are similar:

> How many times did I get hit over the head with that pointer? That was Skite'kmuj's class where she hit me so hard she even broke the pointer. And oh my God, my head used to be so sore. And I couldn't communicate with anyone in the outside world because our letters telling about the mistreatment were read and we were told, "How dare you complain to anyone about this school and how you are treated here. Some of you are lucky you have a roof over your head."

Even when they had nothing in their hands, those in charge had ways of physically punishing children which are still bitterly remembered. Ears were a favourite target. One man remembers the intense pain: "Jesus! I used to hate them earpulls—your ear would feel like it was going to pop off—it would hurt right in the centre core. They used to like to pull ears and twist." I remember that a number of children used to have nearly permanent sores at the top and bottom of their ears as a result of this technique of pulling and twisting ears. It seemed that the nuns' hands could flash out with amazing speed and grasp a handful of hair from behind, jerking the child's head back in a quick whiplash, or fingers could grab a piece of loose skin on the face or throat and startle the victim with the sudden intense pain of pinching and twisting. Another form of punishment was to be locked alone in a room. One girl became so tired of being locked in the bathroom day after day that she managed to take off the door hinges and even swallowed the screws in a desperate attempt to prevent the door being replaced and her punishment repeated.

Much of the time children were being punished, not for deliberate naughtiness, but for behaviour they would have avoided if they could. Wetting the bed was considered a major crime. Besides the usual strappings, they were humiliated in front of everyone. Alice Paul remembers: "Dorothy was made to stand on the table while the nun asked her, 'Does Sister like you?' and when she answered, 'No,' the nun asked, 'Why?' and the little girl replied, 'I peed the bed.' " Nora Bernard's brother was systematically humiliated for bed wetting: "My brother had a problem of bed wetting. They forced him to put on a girl's dress and parade in the refectory in front of all the children and me and my sisters had to sit there and watch his humiliation. I don't know why I didn't run away. Maybe it's because I was the oldest in the family and had to look out for my brother and sisters."

The most enduring and unyielding law was the one that forbade the speaking of Mi'kmaw even during play. None of the nuns knew any Mi'kmaw or made any effort to learn it beyond two words— *Pa'tlia's* [priest] and the term for nun, *Aniap*. [Aniap is a short form of *Aniapsit* which means, "to do penance" and *Aniapsuinu'skw* which means, "a woman who goes around doing penance," while the word for priest has its roots in the French word, padre.] Mi'kmaw was the only language understood by nearly all the students when they first came to school. The few students who were not fluent in Mi'kmaw generally had non-Native mothers or had gone to white schools off the reserves. By the time they were discharged, most of the students had lost their language.

Nancy Marble says: "We weren't allowed to talk Indian. Sister just told me that I wasn't allowed, and when I told her I couldn't speak English, she told me that I had to learn. After a while, I caught on I guess. But I never forgot my prayers in Indian. Some people still pray in Indian but not very many." Joe Julian remembers:

> I got tired of getting hit over the head so I thought I better stop talking Indian and learn English. I don't know what they were. Were they prejudiced or sadists? They liked to inflict pain. They thought that we were savages from the wild and it took me a long while to find myself. I used to work with white people sailing on the great sea but still I can't trust them. I still don't, that's just the way I feel.

One day during my first year, I came into the recreation hall to find Wikew slapping a little girl and yelling at her. The nun had the little girl backed up against the presses which were shelves where we kept shoes, mitts, and our precious junk boxes. The little girl was looking in her junk box when the nun came up from behind her and swung her around and began beating her up. From where I was standing by the toilet door, I could see the nun's back. Her arms were swinging. At first, the nun's size obstructed my view but it also blocked the girl's escape. When Wikew hit with her right hand, her black veil swung left and when she slapped with the right, the veil went in the opposite direction. I could see the girl's feet. At first, she was standing with both feet on the floor, then the Sister pinched her cheeks and her lips were drawn taut across her teeth and her eyes were wide with terror. I stood hypnotized with fear. I had never been so scared in my whole life before and I almost voided a puddle right there on the spot. Then the nun picked the little girl clean off the floor by the ears or hair and the girl stood on her tiptoes with her feet dangling in the air so that one of her shoes fell off. The nun was yelling, "You bad, bad girl." Then she let go with one hand and continued slapping her in the mouth until her nose bled. The little girl was still holding her junk box, while tears and drops of blood were falling in it. Wikew hit the box, and the girl's precious possessions went flying in every direction onto the floor. Suddenly Wikew turned around and screeched at us who were standing paralyzed with fear. "Get out you little savages and don't let me hear anyone else talking that mumbo jumbo again." We all went scrambling up the cement steps that led into the yard. Out of nowhere came Susie. She pushed me gently and firmly out the door. I couldn't even imagine what the little girl had done. When we got out of hearing from everyone else, she told me, "Don't talk Mi'kmaw, Aniap has spies." The next day, I saw the little girl. She had bruises on both cheeks and on her throat where Wikew had pinched her, and her lips were swollen with a cut on the upper one. When one of her little friends tried to comfort her, Wikew called out, "Get away from her, she's a bad girl and if I see you near her again, I'll give you the same thing." When little children first arrived at the school we would see bruises on their throats and cheeks that told us that they had been caught speaking Mi'kmaw. Once we saw the bruises begin to fade, we knew they'd stopped talking.

Although many of those who so relentlessly punished the children entrusted to them are now dead, the effect of their savage punishments has outlived them. Not only were little children brutally punished for speaking their mother tongue, reducing them to years of speechlessness, but the Mi'kmaw language was constantly referred to as "mumbo-jumbo" as if it were some form of gibberish. The ruthless banning of Mi'kmaw in the school drove a wedge between family members. Freda Simon, for example, remembers that when she arrived at the school two years after her older sister they were completely unable to communicate with each other since Freda spoke only Mi'kmaw and her sister spoke only English. The punishment for speaking Mi'kmaw began on our first day at school, but the punishment has continued all our lives as we try to piece together who we are and what the world means to us with a language many of us have had to re-learn as adults.

CHAPTER 5

GHOSTS AND HAUNTINGS

Many students who attended the school feel that it was literally haunted and can find no rational explanation for some of their strange experiences there. Many more are haunted by memories of the inexplicable cruelty they witnessed. One man who attended the school in the late 1950s can never forget the sight of a tiny orphaned baby the nuns were taking care of whose crib stood by the door of the boys' dormitory:

> That poor baby—always crying, always filthy—always crying—we used to touch the baby as we went by. When the nuns weren't looking or weren't around we'd try and comfort it. That's the one thing that really sticks in my mind—that little crib right by the door. I felt so sorry for him. Constantly crying. The nuns would come and slap him—all in the name of God—the Sisters of Charity.

From the very beginning, stories circulated that the school was haunted. From time to time the Bishop would come down from Halifax and bless the whole building. He would lead a procession praying and sprinkling holy water. He was followed by Father Mackey, the ten nuns and all the children. Despite these efforts, most of the children who attended the school can recall some sort of eerie happening. The school had a spooky atmosphere even when nothing particularly odd was going on. Meeting a nun at night in one of the dark corridors was especially scary. I never heard them walking—then suddenly a black-robed figure with a white cap and collar would come out of one of the many doors and appear in front of me. More frightening still was the glimpse of a black figure disappearing into another room because I was never sure whether I was imagining it or not.

One of the things that scared me most as a new arrival was the strange smiling clown faces that I would see staring down at me in bed every night after lights-out. I just stared back until I fell asleep, thinking that if I looked away they would come down and get me. But they just kept smiling as if they were mocking me. When Sister moved me to another bed in another row, I didn't see the faces anymore. Other children saw other kinds of figures which seemed to mock them. Rita Howe recalls that many children saw a little man dancing on top of the presses at night and that it was already a well-established story in the school when she first went there:

> When I first went to the Residential School in 1946, the story was already going around about the little man whose eyes lit up while he was dancing on top of the presses at night. We were all afraid to go to the bathroom after dark because someone said the little man would get us. This character was created by kids who were frightened and it represented their fear and the fact that he was dancing indicated that he was making fun of them.

In the girls' dormitory a frequent phenomenon which seemed to panic the nuns nearly as much as the children was the way that the tall closets which we had been taught to call the "presses" would swing open at night, despite the fact that their doors were secured with swivelling latches. I'd hear the floor squeaking, like footsteps walking along in front of the presses. In the morning, when we got up for Mass, the presses would still be open. Someone told the Sister that the press had opened during the night and when she asked who opened it we told her that it was a frequent occurrence and that nobody had opened it. "The next time you see those presses open during the night, you knock on my door and we'll get to the bottom of this." One eerie night, the wind was softly blowing through the open window and footsteps started walking along the front of the presses. Rosie and I were sleeping in the front row, and the footsteps walked right at the foot of our beds and went right by, down to the end of the dormitory. I was closing my eyes really tight and lying very still trying to ignore them when Rosie shook my shoulder and whispered in a scared voice, "Isabelle, Isabelle, wake up. Look at the presses opening. Somebody just went by and the presses opened." I looked up and one of the press doors was slightly ajar even though they had the kind of knob you had to turn to open the door. All I could see inside the press was darkness. No form. Nothing. A girl in the back row whispered, "Wake Sister up. Knock on her door." I could hear Sister's sleepy voice behind the door. "Yes, what is it?"

"You told us to wake you up when the presses opened. The presses are open."

"Okay, wait a minute. I'll be right there."

For once, I forgot how terrified of Wikew I usually was. Her voice that night sounded like an angel's coming to fix everything and put it all right again. When she appeared, she walked directly to the press and asked, "All right, who's the smart aleck who climbed up here and opened the press door?" And while she was facing us, the door behind her opened just a little bit. She turned around and asked, "Is it my imagination or did this door open just now?" And we all chorused, "The door opened." "Mother of God, help us," she prayed. "The souls in Purgatory need our prayers and those of you who are awake, (which was everybody by this time) kneel by your beds and let's pray for those who have died and who need our prayers." And we all began to echo the words she prayed:

"Out of the depths I have cried unto thee O Lord. Lord hear my voice."

To me the prayer sounded even more scary than the footsteps because I wasn't sure what the word "depths" meant. I imagined that we were in those dark dank depths—crying out for God to listen to us. And there was the nun's figure walking back and forth where the footsteps had walked just a couple of minutes before. The dormitory was dark but a light shone from her door and cast an eerie shadow on the floor as she walked back and forth holding her rosary and praying. All of us girls dressed in nightdresses kneeling on the cold floor were shivering either from the cold or fear, or a combination of the two, glancing over our shoulders occasionally toward the press door which the nun had slammed shut. Once in a while, Sister would stop the rosary and describe the souls burning in Purgatory. The next day, the priest blessed the dormitory by sprinkling holy water all around, and everything remained quiet for about a year when another series of footsteps and opening presses had to be dealt with.

Betsey Paul remembers similar unexplained events:

> God Almighty that place was haunted! If it wasn't one thing, it was another. I felt my bed shake many times and somebody walking towards me. Always somebody going between beds and shaking them. It seemed like your bed was crumbling or shaking or something like that.
>
> Rita Pictou is the one who told me about the knockings in the presses. "Maybe someone is trying to scare us," I said. "No, around about midnight, on a full moon night when the whole dormitory is all lit up, you can see for yourself." The dormitory had many windows with no curtains, just window blinds, and this one night, we both stayed awake to hear the knockings. I got tired and dozed off because I didn't hear anything. Then all of a sudden, I heard this great big knocking—BANG, BANG, BANG. Oh my God, the ghost is here but I wasn't too scared because everything was lit up, so I bravely got out of bed and saw the open press door and I thought that one of the girls had climbed up there. So I crawled back in bed. Then I heard it again, bang, bang, bang. Out of the darkness came Rita's whisper, "See, what did I tellya? The ghost is here." And then the girls who had heard the knockings started waking up other girls, "Are you awake, are you awake? The ghost is here."

Rita Joe suggests the reason why we heard so many knockings and saw so many apparitions was because we were putting it into each other's minds: "I know when I was there, other children often saw something that I did not see. Maybe I did not want to see it. Once we were walking down the hallway when one of the girls asked me. 'Do you see what I see?' I looked in the direction she was pointing and said, 'No, I think I see it, but I'm not sure.' She said it was a man kissing a nun."

While some of these occurrences may well have been the result of active imaginations stimulated by the daily stress of life in the school, others still defy explanation. Betsey Paul recalls one such event:

> Bridget Ann Paul and I were working in Sister Cyprian's

classroom one dark rainy miserable day. Sister was nice and always had a smile for us, and she came in, sat down at her desk and began correcting papers. Next to the classroom was a reading room with a piano in it which was always kept locked and which the children were not allowed to touch, but which we used to pick open with a bobby pin because we wanted to learn how to play it so bad. All of a sudden this piano started playing—dum-da-da dum-dum. It was playing real nice and it was strange because we knew that no one plays that well except Sister Eleanor Marie and she was nowhere around. Sister Cyprian said to me, "Go next door and see who's playing that piano." There was no light on; it was dark in there. So I turned on the light and saw that the lid was closed. There was nobody in sight so I turned off the light and went back to report to Sister Cyprian. No sooner had I picked up my broom when the piano played another melody. The nun looked at me and told me to check again and I said, "No Sister, you go." But she didn't go. Instead, she told me to keep the door open so she could catch the boys who were playing tricks on us. This time the piano played again—la-de-da-dadadadadadum. It was like a slow waltz going up the scale and down again. It sounded beautiful. This time she said, "There is somebody in there playing the piano. Come," and the three of us went to check and when Sister turned on the light and tried to open the piano lid, it was locked.

Another time, Sunday school was in session when the front door bell rang. I was sitting in the front desk in the front row because I was the smallest one in class and whenever something was going on in the hall, my classmates expected me to look out and report back. When the bell rang, everyone stopped what they were doing and looked puzzled because it was such an unusual thing to happen in the middle of the afternoon. Father Mackey had a strict rule not to have any interruptions during class hours. Sister Adrian sent a boy to answer the front door. Then she stepped out into the corridor to knock on Sister Superior's door and ask her, "Are all your students in today?" And after a quick check, it was clear that nobody was missing. And while they were standing around asking each other the same question, "Who could that be in the middle of a Sunday afternoon?" I jumped up from my seat and peered out the door to see what was going on. I saw Sister Cyprian standing outside of her classroom at the other end of the corridor with a questioning look on her face. The three nuns were asking each other if anyone from their class was missing but no one was. With hushed voices, they were asking each other if they heard the doorbell ringing. The boy they had sent to open the door for the guest came back all out of breath and reported, "There's no one there."

Then one of the nuns said, "Well, somebody must have rung the doorbell, it can't ring all by itself. Maybe Father answered the bell and let someone in, I'll go check." She took off down the hall at top speed with her veil trailing behind her. I ran back to my seat and told everybody, "Nobody rang the doorbell." But by this time, everyone had seen the nuns were acting strangely, whispering and going in and out of their classrooms. Everyone was in an uproar because they knew it was *skite'kmuj* [a ghost]. Then Sister Superior came out of the priest's office with her face pale and out of breath said, "Father is not in his suite." Sister Adrian turned paler than the *skite'kmuj* she was named after and asked, "Isabelle, are your parents coming today?"

"Yes, Sister, but they're not allowed to come before 3:30."

For a moment, she looked as if she didn't know what to do. Then she recovered and sent one of the older boys to check the grounds. After a minute he came running back, with a puzzled look on his face, saying, "There's no one out there. I even looked behind the trees on the lawn." Then Sister Superior said, "Somebody needs our prayers and we'd better pray for the souls in Purgatory." And so we all filed into the church and prayed "Out of the depths . . . "

Some have suggested that there may be a connection between these strange experiences and the fact that the school was built on a site which had long been of cultural significance for the Mi'kmaq, or on a former Mi'kmaw burial ground. There is one account that when the site was excavated for building, human bones were found. Most of the stories of odd phenomena, however, seem to have more to do with events that took place in the school itself.

Some children's recollections of eerie events are closely associated with the intense psychological stress they experienced.

I was in the small girls' dorm and my bed was right by the door. I woke up one night and saw myself right off the bed. I could see my bed was on the floor but I was up—above the bed. And I screamed and cried and I screamed some more and the nun came running out and I was put down again. I tried to tell the nun, "I was up." And she said, "Oh, you're just dreaming." I said, "No, I wasn't dreaming. I was up." But she didn't believe me.

One former student recalls that the physical symptoms he suffered after his father died were accompanied by peculiar psychic phenomena:

I used to suffer from stomach cramps when my father died—I couldn't sleep. I'd be all doubled up with pain, and then I'd lie back—and I used to see a light. It seemed like this light from the window used to engulf me. I used to be scared to go to sleep. It went on for months and then it would go away again.

Often peculiar things would happen in the midst of the most ordinary tasks. One student remembers:

Everyone was given chores after supper and four girls were usually assigned to folding bedspreads. One evening they went running up the four flights to the girls' dormitories and when they opened the door, they saw a girl folding spreads in the third row of the little girls' dormitory and they could see the wall and windows right through her.

Other people say that they heard a baby crying. A man who worked at the school for many years was walking his dog behind the school long after it had closed down.

When I came to the boys' side, I heard a child crying, "Mamma, Mamma." Even my big German shepherd stopped what he was doing and looked around. I looked up at the infirmary windows even though I knew the school was empty

for over twenty-five years. I swear to God, I thought I seen
a boy looking out one of the windows. I didn't tell anyone
because I knew they would say I was going nuts.

While the school was still operating some children saw or heard
ghost children in the building. Bernie Knockwood remembers how he
reacted:

> Late at night, after everyone was in bed, I'd hear children in
> the stairway. It sounded like in the morning when all the kids
> were going down the stairs—noisy and relaxed and carrying
> on. I'd lay there and listen to them all night. It only hap-
> pened at certain times and I never figured out why. One
> night, I started down the stairs. When I was half way down,
> it got real quiet. Emerson and I sneaked over to the door and
> we could hear somebody crying, "Kiju', Kiju'." I don't know
> who it was. This happened three times. The third time it
> happened I sat there and prayed for the little boy and said, "I
> hope your grandmother finds you. Be happy." And he never
> came back. Maybe that was the part they were trying to
> quash in us—the ties with our ancestors.

Another student remembered seeing a forerunner of a death in
another girl's family:

> One spring morning when it was just coming daylight, I was
> walking toward Sister Mary Leonard's door to wake her up
> because she didn't hear the bell. I happened to glance around
> to see if anyone else was awake. On Grace's pillow, I saw
> the face of an old man with long white hair. I didn't know
> whether I should go over to the girl and tell her or not. Just
> then she took her blanket and turned around in her sleep and
> covered the old man's face with it. I was so scared I ran back
> to bed. The next day, Grace got word that her grandfather
> had died. He had come to say good-bye to her and what I had
> seen was a forerunner.

Even the nuns were not immune from seeing apparitions. Betsey

Paul recalls:

> Sister Rita taught sewing classes on the third floor which
> was where the choir gallery was located also. She used to
> check every night to make sure all the work was done, and
> one night on her rounds she saw a girl in the gallery but
> didn't stop to talk to her. Then she went downstairs and saw
> the same girl in the recreation hall. "Didn't I just see you in
> the choir gallery?" she asked. And Pauline answered, "No
> Sister, I'm here. You see me now. You must have seen my
> ghost because I'm here now." Sister Rita was so baffled
> because she was so sure she had just seen Pauline some-
> where else.

No wonder we saw or thought we saw ghosts so often. A number
of our class mates died during our school years, sometimes in ways
which suggested to us that our own lives were equally at risk. Rita Joe
remembers the sequence of events which led to Mary Agnes Ward's
disappearance:

> I was in the dining room with Mary Agnes and she asked the
> nun. "May I leave the room." And when she said, "You may
> leave," Mary Agnes said, "Swine." Sister heard her and
> asked her, "What did you say?" and Mary Agnes said, "Nothing."
> So Sister went around asking the girls what she said and
> someone told her, "She called you swine."
>   The Sister took Mary Agnes near the big boys' table and
> began to smack her around, all the while hollering at her.
> She kept smacking her, smacking, smacking until Mary Agnes'
> back was on the boys' table—smack right in the face. The
> other Sister was peering over the fat Sister who was pinch-
> ing and hitting. Mary Agnes struck out, and her right fist
> landed on the other Sister's face. Then the two of them got
> into it. After they were done beating her, the fat one pushed
> Mary Agnes all the way to the scullery and told her to get to
> work. When the kitchen Sister came from the dining room,
> Mary Agnes hid behind the door, but not quickly enough and
> she was seen. "Who is that behind the door?" Mary Agnes

stepped out and you couldn't recognize her because one side of her face was all swollen—her eye, her mouth and nose were bloody. And the kitchen Sister said, "My gosh, what happened to you?" And Mary Agnes couldn't answer so she just puckered up her mouth and faced in the direction of the refectory. The kitchen Sister said, "You march right up to Father Brown and show him what they have done." I was told to leave and I went to the recreation hall and told the other girls what happened. We hid under the open window of the reading room and listened. Father Brown was hollering and talking real loud. He was so angry! It was the first time I had ever heard a priest swear. And we heard her crying. Later when I tried to find out I was told that she was taken to the infirmary on the third floor. She stayed in that infirmary from that time on. Then we heard she was taken to the hospital. Then, sometime later, we heard that she was dead. The incident was so fresh in my mind that when Sister announced that she died because her bones were too big for her heart, I didn't believe her.

Medical records show that Mary Agnes Ward was sent to a TB sanatorium. Whether she died at that time is not documented. For her classmates, her removal to the third floor infirmary after being beaten already threatened her death or permanent disappearance. For us, the infirmary became the place from which children vanished forever. Sometimes we heard that they had died and sometimes we didn't. To us, it seemed that those sick children just evaporated.

When I was researching the school in 1986, I took my daughter Valerie and granddaughter Sisip [short form of *sisipji'j*, meaning little bird] with me to take some pictures. As we drove up the hill, we could see that all the windows in the front were broken, the front door was hanging on one set of hinges and the front of the building had pock marks on its face, where people used to take rifle shots at it. There was no roof and the building was in its last stages of deterioration. My girls jumped out of the car and ran up the stairs while I was still getting my camera ready. They dashed up the flight of cement steps to the front door, but stopped suddenly, turning back to me with a puzzled look. I quickly snapped their picture and went cheerfully up to them saying, "You should have seen the look on your faces." Valerie looked quite scared. "I heard someone whisper, "Come in. You're welcome." "Yes," said Sisip, "Like a nun or a priest." They both had the feeling that someone dressed in black was standing just behind the open door in the shadows.

We burned some sweetgrass and sacred tobacco for protection and then went in. Inside, we found rubbish all over those same floors that the students used to spend so many long hours scrubbing, waxing and polishing. I took them to the chapel first because somehow I was expecting it to be in the same condition as when I was a child. Instead, I found debris everywhere. We walked along the chapel corridor sticking close together and close to the wall because the ceiling was coming down. When we got to the chapel, I told my girls the same thing the nun told my family on my first day as a student, "This is a holy place. And," I added, "a place where a lot of children's prayers didn't get answered." From somewhere in the building, we heard an echo of falling ceilings. "Let's get out of here, Grammy," said Sisip, "before the floor caves in and swallows us up." And after thinking about that for a second, she asked, "What is underneath anyway, Grammy?" I answered, "Used to be a Mi'kmaw burial ground." I looked down at where we were standing and though the floor seemed firm enough I was still worried about falling masonry. I began to realize how dangerous it was and scolded myself for bringing my children into this dangerous place. I told the girls to leave but they wouldn't leave me, so the three of us continued to move cautiously around the decaying building. All of us were trying to make some sort of sense out of this place. We were trying to read the signs from the walls and the windows. The floor that once was so polished and shining was now warped and was slippery from the rotting pigeon droppings. I stood on the platform where the altar used to be and took pictures of every nook and cranny. Then we made our way down the three flights of dark stairways, among the rusted bedsprings and mildewed mattresses on the floors to the refectory where the soap closet was and I snapped three pictures of it before leaving.

Weeks after, I had them developed. On the rotting walls, in the peeling paint, behind the shelves of the infamous soap closet where children were once locked as punishment, I could see the form of a skeleton in a white shadow—skíte'kmuj.

We walked around to the boys' side and that's when we noticed that all the doors of the building had caved in. The chapel windows had been nailed over with some kind of tin sheeting. The tin had gaping holes in it which looked like something had exploded inside and escaped through the windows.

I also took a picture of some graffiti that said, "Burnt in hell, was prison for Indians."

Two days later, the school burnt to the ground and all that was left was twisted steel and charred brick and granite. Only the soap closet, the place of punishment for scores of runaways, failed to burn.

 CHAPTER 6

RESISTANCE

To the Director of Indian Affairs, Ottawa, Canada

————— , 193-

Sir:-

I hereby make application for admission of the undermentioned child into the ————— Residential School; to remain therein under the guardianship of the Principal for such term as the Minister of Mines and Resources may deem proper:

Indian name of child —————————————————————————

English name —————————————————————————

Age —————————————————————————

Name of Band —————————————————————————

No. of ticket under which child's annuity is paid—————————

Father's full name and number —————————————————

Mother's full name and number —————————————————

Parents living or dead—————————————————————————

State of child's health —————————————————————————

Religion —————————————————————————

Does the applicant speak English ?—————————————————

Previously attended ————————— school for —— years

(Signature of father)

Note: If mother or guardian signs, the agent must forward full explanatory note.

I hereby certify that the above application for admission has been read over and interpreted to the parent or guardian and that the contents were understood by him or her and that I witnessed his or her signature on this document:—————————

Signature of Missionary or other witness (Principal or other official of the school must not sign as witness)

I recommend the admission of the above child, who is of good moral character and is eligible to be admitted as a grant-earning pupil.

Signature of agent.——————————————————————

Note: All the above particulars must be fully given, especially the "Name of Band," "No. of ticket under which child's annuity is paid," and "Religion." The minimum age for admission is seven (7) years, except in the case of an orphan, destitute or neglected child. When application is made for the admission of such ages, full particulars should accompany the application.

As children at the school, we always had the feeling that the nuns and especially the principal, Father Mackey, had absolute power over us. But neither we nor our parents knew at the time that when they signed the paper the Indian Agent gave them they were appointing the school's principal as their children's legal guardian even during the summer vacations.

I was five years old and considered "under age" when I was admitted in 1936, so my parents wrote a "special reasons" letter to the Department outlining why I should be accepted: "I find it difficult to provide her with warm clothing, particularly as I am not able to work due to ill health. It will be a healthier environment for her. She will be with her (seven-year-old) sister who can help her in the work." It was signed by my father, though I think he had help with the wording as it was not in his handwriting. I knew nothing about this letter until over fifty years later when I came upon it in the Nova Scotia Public Archives and felt shocked to find that what my father had written as a pleading letter should be a public document for all to see. I also noticed my mother's careful and laborious handwriting of the address on the letter squeezed in at one side of the tiny scrap of paper. The fragmentary document spoke to me about my parents' struggle to teach themselves to read and write. My sister Rosie remembers something of the pain with which my parents reached the decision: "I remember when we were getting ready to go to school. Mom was combing my hair and she had tears in her eyes. She didn't want us to be separated."

Although Father Mackey was given such extensive legal powers, he had trouble with children not wanting to return to the school after summer vacations. Records show that every September he would send a list of missing children to the Department of Indian Affairs asking them to make arrangements for their immediate return.

The Department would send letters out to the Indian agents reminding them that when the parents signed the admission form they had given Father Mackey guardianship over their children even when they were home on vacation. My parents never understood this, which suggests that the Indian agents did not go out of their way to explain the real state of affairs. During the summer vacations and for the two Christmas vacations when we were allowed home, in our own and our parents' minds, we were released from the school's control. Some of the correspondence between Father Mackey and various Indian agents suggests that even some of the agents may not have known how matters stood. In November of 1936 Clarence Spinney, who was the Indian Agent for the Kentville area, wrote to Father Mackey about Pauline Phillips who had been admitted to the Victoria General Hospital in Halifax:

> It would appear to me that Pauline is going to be sick for some time and I do not think the hospital at Halifax is the place for her and I can have this little girl brought from the hospital there and have her removed to the hospital here in Berwick . . . I feel sure she will not be able to go back to school again this fall and winter and her grandfather Isaac Phillips has asked me to have his little girl brought back home . . . he has been to the Victoria General Hospital and seen his little girl and he tells me that all the little girl had on was a little cotton dress and was not getting the attention she should have. Mr. Phillips wishes to have his little girl sent home and placed in a hospital handy to home so he can go see her any time he wishes. Pauline is very homesick and wants to come home, and under these circumstances I have decided that Pauline be sent home and I will have her looked after from this end.

Father Mackey evidently disliked the suggestion that Pauline be transferred from the hospital to which he had sent her or that she should not
return to the school, and he wrote to the Department of Indian Affairs
insisting that the child would probably soon be well. A few days later
the Department wrote to Clarence Spinney to inform him that, despite
his position as Agent, he had no authority in this case:

> It is very possible that you may not know that the pupils of
> an Indian Residential School are wards of the principal dur-
> ing their residence at the school and even during the summer
> holidays when they are home. He is, in effect, their Indian
> Agent, and even more than that, their personal guardian.

The same day the Department wrote to Father Mackey confirming his
absolute authority over the children in his charge. Despite Father
Mackey's optimistic predictions of a speedy recovery, Pauline's illness was found to need a long convalescence and she was sent home.

There were several complaints to the Department of Indian Affairs
both about the quality of education the children were receiving and the
restrictions placed on holidays. Chief Dan Francis of Cambridge wrote
a letter of complaint to the Department stating that the children from
his reserve reported that they were not getting adequate education and
spent most of their time working in the field and doing housework. He
was given a tour of the school and apparently went away satisfied that
the children would receive a good education. On January 1, 1939,
Indian Agent Clarence Spinney of Kings County, wrote to the Department of Mines and Resources, Indian Affairs Branch, Ottawa:

> Dear Sir:
>   The Indians here in Cambridge Reserve were determined
> to have their children who is attending the Shubenacadie
> Indian School—home during the xmas vacation.
>   I refused to grant their request and advised them that
> this was against the rules of the Dept. These people went so
> far as [to] have a man go to the school for their children.
> They did not get the children. Father Mackey would not let
> them take the children.
>   This Mrs. Nibby who you had the letter from thought by

writing she would be able to get her children home for xmas.

These people think they can have their own way and would like to do so and when they find out they cannot they get mad.

I had your rules and regulations regarding this matter.

I remain yours truly,
C.A. Spinney, Ind Agt

In some cases parents or other relatives helped students avoid being sent back to school. Frank and Nancy Marble's parents kept them at home in 1935 after Frank had been whipped by Father Mackey and Edward McLeod the year before. Nancy Marble still remembers Father Mackey bringing the RCMP to the reserve to force her and her brother to return to the school:

Father Mackey brought the cops up to New Town, [a section in Indian Brook] and the old man [Chief John Maloney] didn't allow them in. We seen them coming up through the woods and the old man said, "I'm not going to force you to go back, Tu's (my daughter)," and Mom said, "Run. Run away, run in the woods." And I said, "No, I'm not going to run in the woods. If they grab me, alright." But Frank was more scared than I was and he said he didn't want to go back there because he was whipped and we didn't go back. We went to live with our grandmother in Pictou Landing.

A few parents engaged in time-consuming battles with Indian Affairs to try to free their children from the school. Doug Knockwood's father had to wait for two and a half years before he could get Doug out of the school:

When my father came that Christmas, I had one big shoe on and one little shoe, and snots were running all over my face, and I had a jacket on that was too big for me. He took one look at me and called Father Mackey in and they got into an argument. I remember my father saying, "Take a look at him. When he was home, at least he was hygenically clean

and even though we never had very much he had a decent
pair of shoes on his feet and a jacket that fit. My boys are
coming home with me." Father Mackey told him to get out
so Dad began working on getting us out. His education at the
Residential School helped him to write letters to the bureau-
crats. It took him two and a half years. When you put something down on paper, it's stronger than words. . . . I was so
happy when summer vacation came and I could go home, but
then I was brought back in my second year by the Mounties.
I'm a little nine-year-old boy forced out of my home by the
Mounties and my father is fighting for me not to go back to
that school. My father was a troublemaker for the system
and they took it out on us.

Everyone was keenly aware that it took courage to defy the au-
thorities by helping truants and runaways stay away from the school.
Sulian Herney still remembers with gratitude how his older brother
"literally saved my life" by insisting that he should not go back to
school when he arrived home for Christmas in ragged clothes and
suffering from an infected head wound: "He said I wasn't going
back—he went against the agents, the Mounties, everybody. He saved
my life."

While those who dared to run away were in the minority and still
fewer were able, like Frank Marble, to avoid recapture, many students
risked venturing off the premises for short periods. I remember when
I was fifteen and going to high school, there was a seventeen-year-old
girl there named Mary Clare, whom we called Tiddo. She was on
medication for epilepsy. While the rest of us were in class, Tiddo
tatted and crocheted and read a lot. She was also an excellent story-
teller. One evening, Tiddo approached me and said, "Isabelle, do you
want to go to the movies?"

And I answered, "Yeah sure. When?"

"Right now. I've got the money and Mary Louise is going to open
the bathroom window for us and wait for us and let us back in at nine
o'clock. The movie starts at seven. We'll be back before Aniap misses
us."

"All right, let's go. You got the money?"

"Yeah, I'll pay your way and I even have enough for a chocolate

bar." And away we went. I put my books away and we went down to
the bathroom. Mary Louise took the storm window off and Tiddo
crawled out. Mary Louise had to push me out because I was almost too
fat to fit through it. For a split second, I wondered how I was going to
get back in. Outside the snow was frozen so we left no tracks. Tiddo
started running around the building and I followed. It was dark and the
lights were on in the chapel where the Sisters were saying their
evening prayers.

We ran down over the hill and I looked back to see the whole
school lit up. Every one was doing their evening chores, washing and
drying the dishes, putting little ones to bed, folding down the sheets
for the priest and nuns. I was feeling so privileged for having been
picked by Tiddo to do something wrong because she was such a good
girl, and besides she had money. "Hurry up! The show starts at seven.
You're going to make us late." Tiddo was walking fast and I was
trying to keep up with her. When we got to the Roxy Theatre in
Shubie, we stood in line outside. Then the doors opened and Tiddo
bought two tickets. She handed me one and left to buy a treat. I looked
up and saw one of the white high school students from town watching
us. "Oh God, please don't let him give me away," I was thinking.
Everybody in town knew that we were not allowed out after dark, but
since the whites did not mix with the Indians probably no one would
tell. I followed Tiddo down the aisle and we sat down. I didn't look
back and I didn't tell her that we had been spotted. I was afraid the
excitement might be too much and she'd have a seizure. I glanced over
at her anxiously but she was happily eating her half of the Oh Henry
bar. Then the lights went off and the music started. First there was the
cartoons, then the news, then the previews, but we had come to see
what had happened to Tarzan. Somehow Tiddo had managed to see
earlier episodes and had become a big fan of Tarzan. She wanted to
find out if he had escaped the burning car where he had been trapped
the previous week. Finally Tarzan came on and we found out to
Tiddo's content that he had jumped clear on the other side of the car
just before the explosion. This satisfied her and she grabbed my hand
and said, "Let's get out of here." She ran down the aisle to the side exit
and I followed close behind. We ran all the way back from town, up
the hill and right to the bathroom window. The window opened. Off
came the storm window and Mary Louise in the dark was saying in a

very worried voice, "Sister Mary Leonard was looking for you two."

"Isabelle," said Tiddo, "If she asks, tell her we were in the cellar eating apples, okay?"

"Okay."

"Quick Isabelle, she's in the Sisters' dining room. Get up there and do your homework." I had just sat down when I heard, "Mary Clare?" and another voice answered, "Right here, Sister."

"Where were you? I've been looking everywhere for you." Then I heard, "Isabelle Knockwood, come down here."

'Where were you?"

"I was in the cellar with Mary Clare eating apples."

There were other times when girls ran away to get away for good. Once I was wakened up in the middle of the night by Sister Mary Leonard and Sister Cecily running around with flashlights and talking excitedly. "Isabelle Knockwood, are you awake?"

And when I answered yes, she told Hilda Copage and me to dress quickly and go after Marion and her sister Gertrude. She explained that Sister Cecily had heard a noise in the back window leading to the fire escape and when she investigated, she found three girls attempting to climb out the window. She caught one of them by the shoulders and dragged her back in. The two nuns took Hilda and me to the window to show it to us, as if that was going to help us in our search.

I didn't want to catch anybody, but the excitement of going outside into the nearby field and searching for runaway girls in the middle of the night seemed more like a game of hide and seek to me and Hilda. We were laughing and having fun running down the dark steps, half-afraid and half-excited, pointing our flashlights here and there as we went. When we reached the recreation hall, we ran up the stairs into the yard. Hilda went one way toward the pasture road leading to Snyde's Lake and I took the hayfield. Gee, it was nice! There was no moon but it wasn't dark. There was no traffic, no activity of any kind except insect noises. I could feel the warm night air and smell the hay. Hilda was coming down the tractor path with her flashlight and she called out to me. "Did you find them?"

"No," I yelled back. Secretly I wanted the girls to get away. I was having fun with my flashlight and flashed it around the field in the hay and towards Maitland Road just to see if it looked the same as it did in daylight. It did. I was looking forward to walking down the cowpath to

Snyde's Lake with my flashlight. Instead I heard the nun's voice, "Isabelle, Hilda, come back. You've gone far enough. I don't want anything to happen to you."

I was glad she had called us back because I didn't want to find anyone and I was worrying how I was going to hold onto a girl and take her all the way back over the hill, through the tall hay if she didn't want to come with me. If it had been me, I would have run toward McDonald's farm across the road. Though I didn't find the dark woods attractive, I did get a little excited about being on a search.

The next day, the girls were found and brought back. Their hair was cut short and I assume that they were given the usual punishment of a strapping and a diet of bread and water. Some time later, I was talking to Marion Beadle about it and she said, "If you had kept walking, you would have found me. You were heading right in my direction where I was huddled in the hay. You were so close, I could have reached out and touched you."

Freda Simon remembers planning to run away with some girls, but at the last moment she got sick:

> It was wintertime and we were listening to the weather forecast that night on the radio and I said, "We can't go tonight because it's going to snow." But that very night, I took sick and was given cough medicines and the two girls went ahead without me. But the nuns were waiting for them at the bottom of the hill and brought them back and punished them. . . . We were about eight or nine years old and we were trying to get away from there.

Bernie Knockwood tells the story of one boy who only wanted to see and hug his grandmother because he missed her so much:

> He told me he was going to run away and asked me to go with him but I told him I had no place to go to. "Come with me please. I just want to see my grandmother." But I didn't go. When he got home, they were having a funeral for his grandmother. She died. And they brought him back and beat him.

Joe Julian ran away during the winter of 1938:

> Way back in 1938, in the wintertime, I ran away from that
> Shubie school. I was fed up with them—tired of being hun-
> gry and cold and tired of all of them. John Augustine and I
> took off. We walked and walked toward Oxford Junction.
> We jumped on the train going to Newcastle at five o'clock.
> We rode and rode, God it was late. At last we got to Newcastle.
> We stayed with a couple of people who picked us up and
> after a couple of nights I hitchhiked back to Afton where I
> stayed with Lucy and Johnny Phillips. Then the mounties
> came and took me and Deeodellie [Noel Julian] back to the
> Shubenacadie School. They cut off all our hair and put us in
> the soap closet. I don't know how long they kept this up. I
> guess they kept us in there all night with nothing to eat. Then
> a plate of beans and a slice or two of bread.

Some children managed to run away and never come back:

> When I left, there were three of us. We went down the
> railroad tracks and hid in the boxcars. Some Frenchmen who
> were working there helped us by giving us food and ciga-
> rettes. Eventually I found my way to Portland, Maine, where
> my father and brother Isaac were picking potatoes. When the
> State Trooper found me, my father told them what had hap-
> pened and they told me that I didn't have to go back so I
> stayed in Maine with my family.

Their sister, Hazel, who was fourteen, got away by climbing out
the parlor window on the second floor that was one storey above the
roof of the girls' back door. She then shimmied down the narrow space
between two brick walls in a corner of the building. She told me:

> I followed the railroad tracks to Stewiacke which is about
> ten miles from Shubenacadie. I was cold and hungry and I
> knocked on a white woman's door. She gave me a job and
> promised to pay me at the end of the week, but instead she
> called the police. She never did pay me for the housework I

did for her. I was sent to the Good Shepherd's Home in Halifax which was better than the IRS [Indian Residential School] because at least I had my own room.

Although so many of us made such an effort to escape, the world outside the brick walls of the school was sometimes as terrifying and dangerous as that within. Peter LaBobe knew he would be unable to reach his home in Prince Edward Isalnd and hid in a CNR trackman's shanty until he was caught by the Mounties and brought back to the school. The RCMP truancy report records that he was found "with feet in a bad condition," but the students who were at the school that year remember that he lost his toes to frostbite. Margaret Piero told me that: "The big girls were taken to the infirmary and filed past Peter's bed. His feet were propped up on a pillow and they were badly swollen and purple. There was green colouring between his toes and we thought it was moss. Sister told us, 'This is what will happen to you if you run away.' " Eventually the serious nature of his condition had to be recognized and he was sent to hospital where his toes were amputated.

In the twelve years I was at the school, not one term passed without someone running away. In some years the same child would try over and over again despite the repeated punishments. Many tried to escape by using numerous ingenious ways to get out including: just walking away from the yard during play, jumping out of the second storey windows onto the roof of the back doors on both sides, tying sheets together and climbing down the walls from the third or fourth storeys, using a fire hose to climb down from the dormitory to the ground, using fire escapes, crawling out of basement windows, and in one case filing down a skeleton key to fit all the doors and leaving via the stairway in the middle of the night. Some boys even made keys and raided the storerooms for lunch to take with them.

Running away required advance planning, but some forms of resistance were quite spontaneous. We were generally powerless to resist beatings, but I remember one memorable occasion when someone fought back. One day, Wikew came running down the aisle between the pillars in the refectory and slapped Dorothy Tennasse. She was about fifteen years old, with one more year before she would be discharged from the school. We were all watching fearfully because we didn't know who Wikew was after, especially the girls who sat on benches with their backs turned toward the front. "Aniap," someone whispered as a warning. I breathed a sigh of relief when she whizzed by my table and headed for the big girls' table in the corner. No sooner did she slap Dorothy, than the girl jumped up and slapped her back and also pulled off her veil. The pets all had their lower lips tucked under their front teeth and were inhaling deeply: "She hit Sister and pulled off her veil." The other nun, Chico, as the boys named her, was watching but not reacting much. Finally, she turned her back and told the boys who were stretching their necks to see the happenings, to turn around and eat their supper.

Wikew let go of Dorothy and adjusted her cap. Then she called on her helpers to carry her off to the cold shower. I was scared, but some girls were giggling because they had seen the nun's hair. "She has hair like a man," they were saying. Other kids had a look of indignation on their faces, "She hit Aniap, now she's really going to get it"—a strapping by Father Mackey or a shaved head.

Wikew was standing over her helpers. Two of them were having trouble keeping Dorothy's head under the cold water tap in the deep sink. Her black hair was flying all over her face but was not soaked. She was mighty strong for having beaten off the nun and two girls. Wikew was shouting out orders, "Throw her in the shower and turn the cold water tap on."

The party took off for the showers with Dorothy hanging onto the door frames and sinks along the way with Wikew undoing the fingers and the girls dragging her away. Dorothy never lost her balance, she stayed on her feet the whole time. I was praying silently for her, "Don't fall." That's the secret of successful fighting—stay on your feet. One of the girls, I could see, was trying to trip her, but unsuccessfully. When some of the girls ran after them to the shower room, I went outside and began to cry alone because I felt so mixed up and scared. I walked over to the pasture and began stroking a heifer and feeding it some grass because I needed someone to talk to.

I admired the girls who had the courage to fight back. Some of them tried to give me some tips on how it was done. My friend Leona told me once, "Isabelle, if you ever get a beating, grab the strap." She demonstrated this one day in Ski̇te'kmuj's class by grabbing the strap. You should have seen the look of surprise on Sister's face! You should have seen the look of admiration and surprise on my own face! I was sitting at my desk just shivering with fear. They stood in front of the room, each pulling on the strap until finally, Skite'kmuj went to get Sister Superior who came walking in quietly and said, "Leona, give me the strap," and Leona gave it to her. When Superior left, Leona looked at me and grinned. That's how it's done.

But me—I used to start shivering and biting my nails at the first sign of the strap. I was only a scared little girl—not brave at all, but just waiting for the day when I would get big and could confront Wikew. That day came when I was twelve.

I remember Wikew was going to shave my sister's hair. Rosie was standing in front of her with her head down and Wikew had her left hand on her shoulder and her right hand was holding the electric razor. We were standing in three lines of twos waiting to go to Sunday school.

Suddenly, Wikew flipped the razor on and started to cut Rosie's hair. When I saw the hair falling on her shoulders I realized she was serious. Mostly to get her attention, I yelled "Leave her alone, you big fat pig." And it worked. She stopped, but by this time, she had shaved a strip of about one inch wide and one inch from Rosie's neck up into her hair.

"Who said that?"

"Isabelle Knockwood."

"Who? What did you say. Get over here or you'll get the same."

I walked across the room, but my knees were not shaking for once. Try it, you big fat pig. As I got closer—Boy, she's tall. How am I going to get that razor away from her? Her pets will overpower me so I better act fast. My mind was working fast because I knew that she had the power to do whatever she wanted. By the time I reached her, she had turned off the razor and was holding it over her head and that's when I saw my chance to hit her in the chest. It felt like a pillow. She pushed Rosie away by the shoulder and Rosie took a step backward. Rosie stood nearby with her head bowed down. "Go to bed, you dirty girl." I found out later, she was having her period and didn't know what was happening to her. There were two of us, looking at each other. Her blue eyes were just dilating as if she could see through me. She preached about hitting a nun and scolded me, but I kept my eye and my mind on that electric razor. I thought I was next. Try it pig, I was thinking, I'm telling Mom when she comes this afternoon. I didn't move. I noticed every move in the room—all the girls were watch-ing—not saying a word. Wikew told one of them to sweep up the hair. She was sweeping really close to my feet but I wouldn't move—I couldn't. I was sent to Sister Superior who seemed as if she might be on my side. She sent for Rosie and appeared shocked when she saw her head, but all she kept saying to Wikew was, "Well now, Sister, I'll talk to you later."

When Mom came to visit, Wikew walked in while Rosie's head was on Mamma's lap and Mom was rocking her in the rocking chair. The rest of us were watching them silently, feeling the pain and trying to understand what was going on. Wikew said in a sweet voice with her gold teeth showing, "Mrs. Knockwood, I had to cut your daughter's hair because she did something bad." But what she did bad was never explained. Mom just looked at her in disgust and wouldn't respond. Mom knew she was lying and refused to talk to her after that.

Despite the fact that speaking Mi'kmaw was so absolutely forbid-den, children would use their knowledge of the language to undermine the nuns' authority. Clara Julian could reduce us all to helpless laugh-ter in church when she would take a line from one of the Latin hymns for Benediction, "Resurrecsit sicut dixit" [He said he would rise again]. But Clara would sing at the top of her voice, "*Resurrecsit kisiku piktit*," which in Mi'kmaw means, "When the old man got up, he farted." The whole choir would start laughing and poor Sister Eleanor Marie thought we were laughing at Clara for mispronouncing Latin and she'd stop and patiently teach Clara the proper pronunciation. Clara would just stand there and grin. Even the holy ones had to laugh.

Many of the nicknames we had for the nuns were Mi'kmaw, and even though most of them were insulting, the pets or "squealers" never told any of the nuns what we called them in private. Some of the boys developed nicknames for various nuns based on elaborate and obscene wordplays in Mi'kmaw. During the 1950s one nun who the boys claimed was sexually "loose" was named *Pijikm*—a nonsense word which sounds similar to *Pijeken*—which translates literally as, "throw it in." By the late 1950s the boys had developed their own elaborate "Shubie slang" to such an extent that one man jokingly told me that he's now tri-lingual—able to speak Mi'kmaw, English, and Shubie slang.

A few years after I left school there were two more serious revolts.

On one occasion a group of girls occupied the third floor, locking themselves in and, for once, enjoying some of the food the nuns and priest ate every day. On another occasion a girl hid a knife in her mattress, apparently planning to kill Wikew. The police were sent for and the girl and her sister were both sent to the Good Shepherd Home in Halifax. Strangely enough, the girl who planned the attack was one of the "pets," not one of those who was continually being punished. No one seems to know exactly what provoked the planned attack. However, it may have had some effect, because the following year Sister Mary Leonard's name is absent from the list of nuns working at the school and never reappeared.

Perhaps the most important form of resistance was inside our heads even though it produced little outward sign at the time. Once when Wikew told us, "Don't you dare move a muscle," I was wiggling my toes under the blankets thinking, "You ain't my boss and I'll wiggle all I want." At the same time, I was looking straight at her wearing the Indian mask which I had discovered over the years she couldn't read.

One reward for my years of appearing to be obedient was that I was chosen to go to the local public school. In some ways it was a terrifying experience. Another student from the boys' side was also chosen, but we were given strict instructions not to speak to each other. We walked to and from Shubie village on opposite sides of the road, afraid to speak or even to look at each other. For two long lonely years I walked with my head down from the "Resi" to the high school in Shubie where the post office is located today. Then in the afternoon, I'd walk back again carrying my books. I had the feeling that eyes were always watching from the windows of the school to make sure I did not talk to any of the villagers or go into any of their homes or stores. Even though I spent my time at the Shubie school in complete social isolation as the only Mi'kmaw girl in the school and was far behind the other students in basic subjects, I began to be excited for the first time at the whole idea of learning things.

In my last year at the school, Maimie, Rita and I sneaked off the grounds one day for a while. But we ran into trouble when one of Wikew's pets told on us. The next day while I was in school, my friends were punished. My turn came later when Wikew told me to pull up my skirt and lie across the bench in the recreation hall. A group of girls were standing in a circle watching. All of them were younger than I was, but I did what I was told because I remembered that I was wearing a thick pair of navy blue bloomers that reached past my knees and heavy red knitted stockings. Wikew lifted the strap over her shoulders and came down hard across my buttocks. It didn't hurt because I had such heavy clothing on. She did it again and again and then I stood up. "That's enough," I said. I felt that I had taken my punishment for leaving the yard but to me it really wasn't worth it because nothing happened. Wikew told me to get back down because she wasn't through with me yet and I said, "No." Then I walked over and took my coat and walked out the door. All the girls stepped aside to let me through.

I ran down over the hill and got about fifty yards when a girl came after me and said, "Sister sent me after you. She said that she was sorry and she wants you to come back. She said that the coat is not yours anyway—it was only loaned to you for school." Then she took the coat and started walking back toward the school and I followed her.

Looking back on the incident now I understand even better why I willingly trailed after Wikew's pet even though, at sixteen, I could easily have kept on walking down the hill and never gone back again. Going to the public school had opened up a door, and for the time being, the only way to keep that door ajar was to stay on at the Residential School.

 CHAPTER 7

THE END OF THE SCHOOL

For children who had known no other world than the Indian Residential School, leaving school was a traumatic experience. No thought was given to how they could make the transition to the outside world. For example, when Betsey Paul was discharged from the school at sixteen she was simply given a train ticket to a place she had never known:

> I was given a new dress and new slip with a pair of old ladies' shoes to wear, along with a coat with a fur collar on it. Father Mackey told me that I belonged to the Acadia Band and gave me a ticket for Yarmouth and took me to the train. When I arrived in Yarmouth the conductor told me that this was the end of the line and I had to get off. I got off the train and sat on a bench at the train station which was closed. It was in late evening and I didn't know what to do so I just sat there. A car drove by with some Indians in it, and they looked at me then drove past. I just watched them. Then they came back and stopped. They asked me my name and where I was from. I told them I was from the Indian Residential School in Shubenacadie and that the Indian Agent, Mr. Rice, sent me here with not even a change of clothing and that I didn't know anybody. So they took me home.

When the decision was made to close the school at Shubenacadie some of the the orphan children for whom the school had been the only home felt as if they were being abandoned. One of the last ones to leave was Freda Simon:

> In the last year I was there, they were trying to find homes

for us but they didn't explain why the school was closing. I
had been taken away from my mamma so young and placed
here so it became home to me and when we were leaving I
didn't want to leave. I didn't know if they found a home for
me and I didn't know where they were going to put me. I was
scared. I cried that day we left. It was sad for me. I had lived
there for about two years and it was hard. On the last day of
June in 1967, everyone started leaving slowly. What sad-
dened me the most was to see the parents, uncles and aunts
coming to get their kids and take them home while me and
my sister Doosie sat back and waited to see if they found a
home for us or if my parents were going to come up and get
us. They put us in Truro with the Martins for the summer and
then we were separated. We both went to Whycocomagh, but
I went with William and Janet Syliboy and she went with the
Charlie Bernards.

In August 1967, Mr. Blackburn, a Halifax businessman, bought
the building for a storage place. He told the janitor and cook that their
services were no longer needed. This left only three priests in the
building who were managing on their own by cooking meals on a hot
plate. They lived mostly on sandwiches and canned food. But they
continued to say Mass in the chapel on Sundays and to hear confes-
sions every week. Then Mr. Blackburn came and told the priests that
they would have to leave and gave them twenty-four hours to find
another place. According to someone who was present, the elderly
priest picked up the phone and called the Bishop for instructions. He
was told that there were no places available at the time. The priests
had no place to go. Mr. Blackburn told them, "Take your things and
get out or I'll call my men and they'll put you out." So the priests went
to Indian Brook and stayed with Father Bernardo, the parish priest.

A man who attended the final Mass described how the priests
made their departure from the school:

> The next morning the last Mass was celebrated. After Mass
> was over, the elderly priest took the Chalice containing the
> Blessed Sacrament and carried it down the chapel corridor.
> He was ranked on both side by two other priests. The proces-

sion was made up of some white Catholics from the village and Native people who all followed reverently down the front steps onto the front lawn. There were two cars parked in the front. The young priest took the Chalice and placed it in the trunk of one of the cars. Then both priests took off their stoles, and the younger one put his over the Chalice and the elderly one put his in his pocket. The first car started going slowly down over the hill. Most of the people were walking away. I stood by, waiting for everyone to leave. The older priest seemed distracted at first. He turned back toward the school with tears in his eyes. Then he unfolded his stole and replaced it around his neck. He took a black prayer book out of his pocket and began hitting the palm of his other hand gently with the book and crying. Then he looked up at the building and lifting up both hands as if calling on a higher power, he said. "I don't know if this building was cursed before but no matter what we tried to do, it never turned out right. If we can't say Mass here anymore, I hope to the Holy Mother of God in heaven, that this building is never used for anything else." When he was done, he put the prayer book back in his pocket, and took the stole off his neck. For a moment, he staggered and fumbled with the car door. Then he opened it and got in and the car started up and he drove slowly away.

Within a year, Mr. Blackburn's business deal fell through and he sold the building to a man who wanted to use the bricks, but he soon found out that they were of an inferior quality and crumbled when he tried to work with them. Over the next twenty years the disused building became a hangout for parties. The drinking and toking up on marijuana added to the sinister look of the building at night. In daylight, it was just an old building and everyone took it for granted that it would always be there.

In 1985, a new owner, Herman Juurlink, made an agreement with Ronald Corbin of Dollar Lake to demolish the building in exchange for salvage with which to build a house. On September 4, 1986, Mr. Corbin started a controlled fire in the kitchen. Mr. Corbin's crew watched the fire all day and, that evening, they left around seven o'clock. The fire was still smoldering, but since there were no combustible materials nearby it was considered safe to leave.

During the afternoon, people driving past on Maitland Road saw smoke coming from the chapel area but few took it seriously. One woman told me, "We thought the building was going to last forever."

That same evening, at around 8:30, Peter Robinson, who had worked at the school as a janitor, saw a blast of fire shoot out from the main entrance. The fire spread quickly to the top floor, burning both sides of the building simultaneously, until the whole structure was aflame. The intense heat caused by flash fires bent the steel beams into S shapes. Sparks shot up from the top of the building and lit up the entire night sky. For the first three hours, the fires burned brightly and it appeared as if Spirits were dancing inside the tar and brick. Fire trucks from Shubenacadie, Stewiacke and Windsor arrived, as well as many spectators, whose cars were lined up at the bottom of the hill and along Maitland Road. Most people just watched from their cars. No one ventured too close to the building because of the danger of flying bricks. Many were taking pictures and videos until 2 a.m., when the blaze died down. In the meantime, I had gone to bed early and Ruby Maloney, who had watched the fire after Bingo, called me and said, "What are you doing in bed, don't you think you better get down and get some pictures of the burning school?" Meanwhile, the Snydes, the white people who lived nearest to the school, were watching the fire from their house. "Well, the lights are gone out at the College for the last time," was Doug Snyde's comment.

By the time I and my son Karl arrived, nearly everyone had gone home except for one fire truck and a few people walking around. We went out back and took some pictures. I could hear a series of small explosions that sounded like the canisters used by firemen in fire demonstrations. I hadn't talked to anyone but my first impression was that the fire had been set by the fire department because it was a public safety hazard. The next day I was surprised to read in the *Halifax Herald* that the origin of the fire was undetermined and one possibility was that the Indians had burned it down. The other thing that seemed strange was the fact that neither the RCMP nor Ronald Corbin, who was tearing down the building at the time, was called to the fire.

The next morning, when Mr. Corbin came to work, he was shocked to find that the school had burned down during the night. The con-

I took this picture two days after a mysterious fire destroyed the derelict school building. The wrecking crew finished off the remaining walls.

trolled fire in the kitchen was still smoldering after fifteen hours. The pipes leading from the kitchen to the rest of the building had been broken off months before, so the flames could not possibly have spread by means of vents or pipes. The ceiling next to the kitchen leading to the main building was partially covered with tin plating specifically designed as fireproofing. All the floors on the basement level were made of cement. "No way," he said when I asked him if the controlled fire in the kitchen could have caused the building to burn down so quickly.

Mr. Corbin took my camera and photographed the building from the inside out. The photos showed that the school was divided into four sections, each section separated by an eighteen-inch fireproof wall made from brick and cement. If a fire had started in one section, it could not have spread to the other sections. It seemed strange that a building constructed mainly of steel and brick, rather than wood, would burn so fast. Speculation about the origin of the fire began while it was still blazing that September night in 1986 and has continued to this day.

The charred remains of the building did not stay in place for long. Two days later, on September 6, 1986, almost exactly fifty years since I had watched my parents sign my school registration form, a group of former students of various ages gathered in the Robinsons' back yard at the foot of the hill to have a barbecue and to watch the demolition of the old school. Someone had set up benches and chairs and some were relaxing, sipping beer, while others armed themselves with video camera and binoculars. When Nora Bernard and I arrived, people were all talking excitedly about the power outage. Apparently what had happened earlier that morning was that the demolition truck from the P&H Company in Truro had driven up to the boys' side and started pounding the walls down with a ball and chain. The arm of the truck hit the wire leading to the building which everyone thought had been turned off. Instead, it was live. Sparks were flying in every direction and the two men in the cab were afraid they were going to be electrocuted. Electricity in the town was disrupted for two hours until the linemen came and disconnected the power. Meanwhile, people were beginning to talk about the possibility that the building might be cursed and this set the stage for a day which was to be filled with many emotional events.

I thought about how many of my former schoolmates, like Leona, Hilda and Maimie, had died premature deaths. I wondered how many were still alive and how they were doing, how well they were coping, and if they were still carrying the burden of the past on their shoulders like I was. I was so grateful to have Nora with me that day.

My thoughts were interrupted by the motor starting up and the wrecker swinging back into action. Bang. The ball hit the upper right hand corner of the boys' side and bricks went flying in every direction. The crowd watching from the bottom of the hill cheered, "Hurray!" There was no sadness, no tears at seeing the building finally being punished and beaten for having robbed so many Indian children of the natural wonders and simple pleasures of growing up and the joys of being alive and being Native. In a strange way, the building had taken on an identity all its own.

When the boys' side was finished, the machinery moved to the east wall. Just as they lined up to hit the building, the big iron destruction ball fell to the ground. I looked up to the third floor where the boys' infirmary had been and where very sick children were kept. Sometimes when they were sent there, we never saw them again. When I used to get sick, I wouldn't tell Wikew and tried to recover very quickly before they could have a chance to send me there.

I was thinking of Nancy Lampquin who was sent to the infirmary after receiving a severe beating from Wikew. I was about ten years old and I was sitting in the refectory opposite Nancy who had her back to the two Sisters standing up front. We had spinach that day, which I liked but which Nancy could not eat. She asked me, "Do you want my greens?" I said, "Yes, but wait until Aniap looks away." The nun never took her eyes off me during the whole meal and when it was almost over, Nancy panicked and took the spinach and put it in her pocket. Chico caught the movement of her elbow and whispered to Wikew. Wikew had long since taken off her rosary beads so we wouldn't hear them rattling when she came up from behind us, so Nancy didn't hear her coming and I couldn't warn her because the other nun, Chico, had stepped aside to get a better view until Wikew got there. Wikew came up behind Nancy, grabbed her by the hair and pulled her head back. As her head was jerked back I saw the look that seemed to say, "Isabelle, why didn't you warn me?" I felt so guilty for not having kicked her under the table, but Chico was watching every move. If she could spot the movement of Nancy's elbow, I was sure she would spot the movement of my leg under the table.

Holding Nancy's head back, Wikew was yelling, "What have you got in your pocket?" Nancy mumbled, "Greens." "Take them out of your pocket and put them on your plate." Wikew took a fork and began to cut the spinach in small pieces while the rest of the kids watched. Nancy had her head down and she was crying. Tears were falling in her lap. I was getting really scared now and blinked back my own tears. If I'd been caught crying, I would have been beaten too. Wikew took a spoon and began spooning the spinach into Nancy's mouth. Nancy gagged. The nun pinched her nose and food splattered all over the place, including on my plate and Wikew's face. The nun was yelling, "Swallow it, Nancy, swallow it." Nancy was trying to stop crying so she would be able to swallow, but she couldn't. Wikew just kept shovelling the food in her mouth and hitting her lips with the spoon. Blood and tears and mucus mixed with the greens and Wikew just kept shoving the food in Nancy's mouth until her cheeks were bulging. I was so scared I was shaking and sitting on my hands so no one would notice. Food was gurgling out of Nancy's mouth until finally she coughed and spit all over the nun. This infuriated Wikew. Her face was pink with anger. She forced open Nancy's mouth by placing her thumb on one cheek and her middle finger on the other cheek. Then she grabbed a tin cup of milk and poured it in her mouth. Nancy's eyes began to roll and she seemed to be losing consciousness. Wikew finally took her by the hair and rubbed her face in her plate. The boys were all standing on the benches to get a better view. Some turned away in disgust, while others kept their eyes glued to the spectacle. Nancy's place was cleaned up and her plate was removed and washed in the scullery by one of the girls. Nancy was led out by two girls, one on each arm, to the lavatory to be washed up. As she passed by, she was barely able to walk. Her head was bowed and a mixture of tears and blood was streaking down her face. Her mouth and cheeks were badly swollen and her lips were purple. She was sobbing and gasping for air and holding her back rigid and straight. That is the image that is imprinted on my mind today. I never saw Nancy alive again. The next I heard of her, she was in the infirmary on the third floor. The next day, Wikew removed Nancy's tin plate and told the little girls to move down one place to fill the space where she had sat. She told us in an off-hand manner that Nancy was in the hospital with tuberculosis—the "galloping disease." "They call it galloping because once a person gets it, they gallop toward death and there is no cure," she explained. Everyone remained silent for a long while. That was our memorial to her. We were remembering the severe beating of yesterday but were afraid to talk about it to each other.

That summer Mom asked us if we knew Nancy Lampquin. When we told her we did, she continued, "She's buried up here on the Reserve." We told her what had happened to Nancy and she was aghast. "I didn't think they were like that," she said. Then she exchanged some words in Mi'kmaw with Daddy, suggesting that he talk to Father Mackey. The priest apparently put my father off by pointing out that he wasn't Nancy's next of kin. He said her father was out working on a trapline somewhere in the Quebec woods and could not be located, and the matter was dropped. The next Sunday after Mass, the whole family visited Nancy's grave which was marked with a large wooden cross which read: "Nancy Lampquin, age 12. May she rest in Peace." Since that day, the circumstances surrounding Nancy's death have plagued me. When I went over the school register in researching this book, I found this entry against Nancy's name in Father Mackey's handwriting: "Very delicate and sick for almost a year. Died. "

After the wrecking ball had fallen off, the demolition workers decided to use the crane's arm as a battering ram to push down the walls. While I watched the third floor being pushed in, I remembered a story told to me about how Father Collins had begun his new administration in 1958, after Father Mackey's death, by taking inventory of the storerooms. At the back of the third floor was a storeroom where the shelves were filled with brand new shoes, overshoes, woolen stockings, bedding and towels, and various types of fabrics, all still in their original wrappings. When they were taken out, they were full of holes where the moths had eaten them. Everything came apart at a touch. The clothing had been sitting there since the school was built and had been wasted, while the children had gone without. The previous administrator, Father Mackey, had prided himself on efficiency. When Father Collins was directed to wind down the school's affairs before it closed, he practised his own form of efficiency. Most of the school's equipment was either abandoned or deliberately dumped rather than being put to use. A few people from the Reserves asked for beds and got them. The valuable industrial sewing machines were taken out by the furnace man in a canoe and dumped in the Shubenacadie River on Father Collins' orders. In the final days, he also decided to burn all the school's records. He first asked a Native man who worked as a janitor to make a bonfire of the documents, but he refused because he thought that they were probably the property of the government and that it would be illegal to destroy them. Later in the day Father Collins went to the liquour store and came back with a bottle of rum which he gave to a white man employed to look after the furnace. After drinking some of the rum, the white man made a large bonfire of all the school's records.

In the years when the building had been derelict and ruined I had often wondered why it deteriorated so fast when other brick buildings seem to last for a hundred years or more. I questioned one of my friends in the construction industry who explained that the inferior quality of the building materials led to the building being plagued from the beginning with roof leakages and flooding after heavy rains. Through the years moisture built up between the walls and caused cumulative deterioration of plaster and warping of the hardwood floors. Impressive as the building had once seemed to us, it now appeared that poor materials had doomed it from the beginning.

All afternoon the walls were coming down. By early evening, the heavy equipment had moved to the front lawn on the girls' side where it got mired on the lawn. I was thinking, "I told you, it is cursed." Herman Juurlink, the owner of the building, pushed the truck out with his tractor and the demolition continued. By noon, the whole front of the building was down, including the Sisters' community room on the third floor where a life-size crucifix hung on the wall. I always avoided looking at it whenever I cleaned the floors in there. Some girls used to come in and kiss the feet of Jesus on the Cross and I did too. Just when I was trying to be holy, Maimie Paul would often come in and make me laugh. It seemed that the more she was beaten the more daring she became. Over the years as she grew bigger she would seem to challenge Wikew to hit her, and the more carefree she appeared the more Wikew would want to punish her.

When the third floor fell, the second floor collapsed, including what was once the manual training and pottery room. I enjoyed pottery but although we were allowed to put our initials on the pots we made, we never got to keep them or to give them away as presents. Many years later I found out that our work was sold at agricultural exhibitions. However, we had no idea that this was being done and never saw any of the money.

The whole building was now just a pile of bricks and twisted steel burying what was once the recreation hall in the basement. It seemed that there was always something sinister going on in that room—the pit of our oppression. I was thinking about the number of times I'd seen Margaret Julian punished in that room. Margaret was part-Mi'kmaw and part-Black and seemed to be singled out for special punishment. On one occasion when she was about five or six Wikew poured some flour or powder over her head and face. She was running back and forth in the middle of a circle of little girls who were watching; some were laughing, but most had a shocked, disgusted look on their faces. Two black lines came from her eyes where the tears were running.

When I visited the derelict school, I found this mangle behind the barn. It was used to iron sheets, spreads and tablecloths. Peter Robinson took this picture of me with my hand on the middle roller, which was heated with electricity. The three smaller rollers were padded with asbestos. It's the one my friend Teresa Ginnish got her hand caught in. God, it was awful! I was nine years old when I saw her maimed by this machine. The memory still affects me.

After she was made to run back and forth for a while, Wikew lifted Margaret onto a bench and made her sing,

"Peggy O'Neill is the girl who can steal,
Anytime, anyplace, anyhow."

After that day, Margaret was called Peggy O'Neill by us all. Despite what seemed to be almost daily punishments, Margaret was the one who was always singled out to perform for white visitors. She was even made to sing that same song when white visitors came to the school.

In the early evening, the machinery drove to the back of the girls' side where the laundry door was located. The chapel walls were left standing for the time being. And by this time some townspeople had come to watch. It was as though an invisible line was drawn between the two groups. The white people watched from one side of the fence while the First Nations people and their children watched from the other side. I pointed this out to Herman, "Look, the racial lines are drawn." He said, "Isabelle, why do you always notice these things?" I answered, " Because I was brought up here and I know that Shubenacadie is a racist town." Herman shrugged off my comment, but I thought about how the school had taught us racism long before we even knew the word. The nuns left us in no doubt about our place in the world by the different ways we saw them treat light-complexioned or white children. Nora Bernard, who was standing beside me watching the demolition, had once told me how she felt when watching the nuns care for a white child, the daughter of an Indian Agent brought to the school for two weeks while her parents were on vacation:

> She was always carried around, babied and always showered with love and attention. She was fed the nun's food and slept in one of the infirmary rooms where one of the pets stayed with her. She was put on a pedestal. I used to look at the statues of the Virgin Mary, Saint Anne and Infant of Prague in the chapel and watch how the nuns used to dress them up and carry them around and shower love and attention on them and I used to think, Oh, God, I wish I was light complected so I could be treated like the little white girl who's treated like the statues on a pedestal.

While we all stood around, the sun was starting to set and people were wondering if all the walls would come down before the sun set. When one wall was pushed in, I could see what remained of the grade four classroom. On the blackboard were painted two maxims: "Idleness is the Mother of Misery" and "Be Honest, Truthful, Manly." How I dreaded standing at that blackboard where I felt so vulnerable and defenceless with my back turned. When there were no rulers available, Skɨte'kmuj would grab an eraser and hit kids over the head leaving a big white rectangular spot where the eraser had landed. Every morning arithmetic lasted two solid hours. Still, when I left the Resi, I was ill-prepared for grade nine math. It took me hours and hours of studying to catch up with the non-Native students in my class. Sisters Eleanor Marie and Cecily gave me extra help with my equations and fractions and I finally made a passing grade.

I took these pictures in what remained of the grade four classroom. On the blackboard were painted two maxims: "Idleness is the Mother of Misery" and "Be Honest, Truthful, Manly." How I dreaded standing at that blackboard where I felt so vulnerable and defenceless with my back turned.

By nightfall, all that was left standing was the archway and the thirteen steps which had led to the front door. The first rooms on the right had been Father Mackey's suite. When he finally died in May 1957, he was laid out in an expensive coffin in the main parlour. Peter Julian was among the students who had to pay their last respects:

> We had to line up and go to the front parlour to pay our last respects to the priest who had abused us. All the children were forced to say their prayers . . . I didn't pray. I just knelt there and I was sort of happy. I've never been so happy over a person's death in my life. I was kneeling there feeling kind of glad that he was dead and that it was finally over . . .

Although it was held in Springhill, only an hour's drive from Shubenacadie, no one except the Chief, John Bernard, attended the funeral.

It was quite dark now and my mood was changing because I was being haunted by memories of my mother's soft voice on my first day, when Susie took me down the dark steps leading to the recreation hall, and I thought I could hear her saying, "Take good care of my children."

CHAPTER 8

THE OFFICIAL STORY

If I had never attended the Indian Residential School and had based this book on material in libraries and archives, rather than on the students' own experiences, I would have told a quite different story. The photographs accompanying newspaper accounts of the school show rows of smiling neatly-dressed children. The newspaper stories refer to "this fine institution" run according to "humanitarian and democratic principles." I remember how we used to have to change our prison-style, broad-striped blouses for dresses on the day of the photograph. Then we lined up in rows according to height with Wikew yelling, "Smile, smile," as the photographer snapped the picture.

As students we all knew that a special show was put on whenever the school came into contact with the outside world. The monthly letters home were written in class, and anyone who wrote anything critical about the school was punished and made to rewrite the letter, leaving out their complaints. Imelda Brooks remembers that, although she had no warm outdoor clothes at school, she was dressed in a new snowsuit and boots to go to medical appointments in Halifax:

> I had doctor appointments in Halifax for my polio. Sister Gilberta would take me there. I told her I was going to tell the doctor how we were treated. All through the examination, she dug her nails into my shoulder and said I would get the strap. I was scared so I never said anything. Of course, when we got back, I got the strap . . . The only time I had a nice warm new snowsuit and boots was when I had doctor appointments.

Showing off the school to visitors involved much more preparation. Nora Bernard remembers:

> Every time any officials came from the Department of In-
> dian Affairs, or a special visitor like Mother Superior or the
> Bishop, the meals would be different. We'd be served cornflakes,
> and oranges and toast for breakfast and the tables would be
> set up so nicely. They always knew when the officials were
> coming so they had time to cream it up. If the inspectors had
> come unexpectedly, they would have caught them at their
> game.

Those of us who went home during summer vacations presented a risk
to the school's public image. I remember Sister Superior coming into
our classroom to lecture us about loyalty to the school and how it was
our responsibility to keep its reputation good and not bring disgrace to
it and to Father Mackey. "You give the school and your teachers the
same loyalty you give your parents. For example, you don't go around
telling the whole neighbourhood when your parents have a fight so
you do the same thing here. Don't repeat what you've seen and heard
about the fights or punishments in the school especially when you go
on vacation because we have ways of finding out if you do." Efforts
were made to control any accidental contact we might have with the
outside world. Father Mackey used to make frequent trips to the
Indian Brook Reserve to draw water from the pump for his personal
use because he refused to drink the water that came from the school's
pipes. He would generally take two or three students with him to carry
the water. Marty Bernard, who was a small boy at the time, remembers
Father Mackey giving orders to the children living on the Reserve,
"Don't talk to my students. They are not allowed to talk to anyone."
  Occasionally the efforts at creating a good reputation for the
school provided some enjoyable spinoffs. When Sister Eleanor Marie
became Sister Superior she organized a concert at the school to mark
Father Mackey's Silver Jubilee in the priesthood. We were all taught
Scottish dancing and took to it with enthusiasm. After school the girls
would practise dancing—put your hands on your hips and: "Toe, heel,
toe, kick with the right foot, then again with the left foot, then side
together, back, front." The dance caught on, and everywhere girls and
boys were singing and dancing in the yards, in the halls, at every

Father Brown poses with students in front of the school.

opportunity. On concert night, they were dressed in Scottish plaid because of Father Mackey's Scottish ancestry. Everything went well. The Bishop and the Indian Agent, Mr. Rice, and his family were all sitting in the front row, and all the nuns were walking around with smiles on their faces.

Some students echoed the nuns' presentation of the school. This is what one student in grade six wrote in class when the school was about to be closed:

> From the first years that I came to the Indian Res. School I liked the school very much. I can think back to the times that Sister Gilberta gave us candy and other good things. I am very thankful to her. The Sisters all take very good care of us. But now that the school is closing I don't know what I am going to do without the Sisters. We get a full supply and good food and plenty of sleep each night and lots of fun. The Sisters teach us manners and how to act like little ladies. I'm

very sorry that this school is closing up. It wouldn't be
closing up if it wasn't for the Boys and Girls that had run
away. They gave the school a bad reputation and told the
people all kinds of tales about how they were treated here.
But they were very mean to say that. They even spoiled it on
all the Boys and Girls who have no homes to go to. I really
hoped that this school wouldn't close. I know we are all
going to miss it very much.

This account, which seems to be the only school essay preserved in the
Sisters of Charity's archive, is quite similar to the ones I have received in correspondence with some of the nuns. Some of them acknowledge that too severe punishments were meted out, but suggest
that this was only a personal failing of an individual. Some blame the
nun we called Wikew, who seems to have had "Mistress of Discipline"
as her official title, though I don't remember ever hearing her called
that. Another nun to whom I had written about the interviews I had
recorded, responded that she found, "so much ingratitude, exaggera-
tion and negative remarks in what you have been told. What about the
meals, clean clothes, and care that was given when they were sick?
Any out of the way punishments that were meted out was not the
choice of those that spent long hours in the recreation rooms. They
came from the Principal. So why not put the blame where it belongs?"
None of the nuns with whom I corresponded seems to have had any
serious criticism of the institution itself.

The public relations efforts of the school seem to have been very
successful. White people who lived near the school have told me,
"We thought you kids had it made." The frequent attempts at escap-
ing from the school which were reported in the newspapers do not
seem to have prompted outsiders to wonder if children were unhappy
or ill-treated at the school. When they appeared in the papers, these
stories were told as accounts of successful pursuit and capture, not as
indications of children in terrible distress. For example, in 1939,
when the RCMP began to use a dog to hunt down runaways, both the
RCMP official report and the news story focussed on the dog and not
the child. The Doberman, P/D K 27, and known to his handlers as
"Perky," was lavishly praised in the police report, "One may consci-
entiously state the results obtained by Ct. Boland and P/D K 27 was

most gratifying . . ." After the capture of two boys, one of whom was treed by the dog after managing to get as far as South Maitland, the *Halifax Herald* ran a story with the headline: "First assignment success: Police dog finds missing Indian boys," praising the efforts of the dog:

> A Royal Canadian Mounted Police dog, placed with the Halifax detachment one month ago for tracing criminals and lost persons, quickly crowned his first official "assignment" with success Saturday when it located two students who had run away from the Shubenacadie Indian School a few hours after they had left the Hants County Institution.
>
> The 30-month-old Doberman Pinscher found the escaped Indian boys at different points deep in the backwoods, some seven miles from the school, after a chase with his master-trainer through brush and across ploughed fields and a frozen lake.
>
> According to police officials, the pupils left the school at 6 a.m., walked five miles together and then parted company in opposite directions.
>
> A piece of clothing of one of the boys, aged 12 and 13 years, gave the police hound his scent which started him on the search. Six and one-half miles from the institution the first boy was found. The dog was then returned to the RCMP detachment for a rest and was started off again with a shirt belonging to the second pupil.
>
> The hound followed the original trail for five miles, then turned in a direction opposite from the one the other lad had taken when the two parted. The second boy was found a distance of 3 1/2 miles off the main trail.
>
> RCMP officials, who kept secret the hound's joining the Nova Scotia division until his first real trial, expressed pleasure last night at the results of his work and believed he would prove a major help in finding persons becoming lost in the woods in the future.
>
> The dog is one of some 33 used by RCMP in their work across Canada, it was said.
>
> He will only work with his trainer who joined the force approximately at the same time he did and subsequently was

transferred with him to Nova Scotia as a constable after the
hound had received a 13-month course at Regina training
headquarters.

The school certainly had no trouble in receiving favourable press
reports even when there was every reason to be suspicious of how it
was run. The most striking example of this is the press coverage of the
public hearing which followed the flogging of nineteen boys in 1934.

It appears that some boys had managed to steal $53.44 from a cash
box in Sister Superior's office. They had then sneaked out through a
window at night and spent the money in Shubenacadie on cake, bis-
cuits, gum, candy, tobacco and jackknives which they proceeded to
share with other children when they got back to the school. When the
theft was discovered on Saturday, March 17th, Father Mackey began
questioning the boys he suspected and called in Constable Thurston of
the RCMP. It seems that they failed to identify the real culprits by
means of their interrogation and that the decision was made to thrash
all of the boys who might have been involved. Edward McLeod, the
school handyman, was given the task of making a special strap for the
occasion. He made a seven-thonged strap from harness leather with
knots in the thongs. Father Mackey had been suffering from a sore
throat and after the exertion of flogging the first boy he passed the
strap to McLeod who flogged the other seven boys while the RCMP
officer looked on. Their punishment was continued by being put on a
bread and water diet for the next five days. Meanwhile Father Mackey
continued to interrogate other boys he thought might be implicated in
the theft, or at any rate, "sticking together." On Wednesday he thrashed
another eleven boys, this time without McLeod's help.

Precisely what happened next is hard to unravel from the official
accounts. One person who lives in Shubenacadie told me that some of
the boys ran away and reported their injuries to the Indian Agent who
was working in a field near the school property at the time. The
records show that the Indian Agent, Allison MacDonald, reported the
incident to Indian Affairs as a formal complaint.

Evidently MacDonald's complaint became public knowledge and
even resulted in questions in the House of Commons. An opposition
party MP, John Livingstone Brown (Lisgar, Ontario), questioned T.G.
Murphy (Neepawa, Manitoba), the Minister of the Interior and Super-

intendent-General of Indian Affairs, about the "barbaric" treatment of the boys, based on reports he had read in newspapers. Clearly there had been a good deal of public discussion of the incident, since the Minister immediately responded by saying that a commission of inquiry was being set up. A few days later, on May 9th, 1934, the government announced the appointment of L.A. Audette, a retired judge of the Exchequer Court of Canada, as a royal commissioner under Part Two of the Enquiries Act. Audette was already seventy-eight at the time of his appointment. Nothing in his career to that point indicates any interest or expertise in Native issues or any experience in criminal law.

When the hearing was held a month later it was covered extensively in the press. *The Halifax Herald* gave the most detailed account. The report gives the impression that the hearing made an entertaining spectacle for local people in Shubenacadie, who overflowed the hall. The "goodly sprinkling of Indians" who had walked the five miles from the reserve and "who stood grouped behind their leader, Chief John Maloney" are described as adding "a picturesque touch," while the "brilliant red uniform" of Constable Thurston was "reminiscent of frontier days." When a witness testified that the boys who had been placed on a bread and water diet for four days "added to this frugal fare with stolen milk and more bread," a "ripple of amusement went around the hall."

When they gave evidence, Father Mackey, Constable Thurston, and Edward McLeod are reported as having "stoutly denied the boys had received excessive punishment." Evidently this denial was accepted by both the Judge and the newspaper despite the fact that medical testimony showed that seven of the ten boys examined on the day of the hearing still had marks on their backs from the flogging they had received three months earlier. Joe Toney was ordered to bare his back in the courtroom revealing "a series of five or six pencil width blue markings." The newspaper report, however, goes on to remark that Toney was "sturdily built" and cites his height and weight. No mention was made of the fact that the youngest boys who were beaten were only about a third of Toney's size—the school's medical reports for that year list one of these boys, John Augustine, as only fifty-five pounds, with three of the other boys in a similar range. No-one seems to have been concerned that thirteen-year-old Matthew

Thomas was also beaten despite the fact that he had had major surgery nine weeks earlier when he had had a kidney removed. Father Mackey's testimony that there, "was no evidence . . . to show the boy suffered any ill effects from his beating," seems to have been completely accepted by the court.

Reading the newspaper report, it is hard to imagine what kind of punishment would have been found "excessive" by those in charge of this inquiry. When the strap was produced, three of its seven thongs were missing. "Father Mackey said one had fallen off while a boy was being thrashed and two were pulled off because they were barely hanging." This evidence seems to have caused no speculation about what kind of beating would tear apart horse harness leather. Both the Judge and the reporter seem to have been satisfied by Mackey's account:

> Mr. Justice Audette: Were there any agonizing screams?
> Father Mackey: No, Your Lordship.
> Judge Audette: They took it stoically?
> Father Mackey: Yes. One boy whimpered.
> Mr. Hanway: What force was used?
> Father Mackey (A slight man of medium stature): Well, I'd say it wasn't anything like I could use. I do not want to injure any boy in any way at all.

Father Mackey also denied that the strap had been soaked in vinegar to increase its sting. The evidence which he produced for this was the strap itself "which bore no signs of having been dampened." No one seems to have considered that the strap was not likely to have remained damp from March to June. But there was no one taking part in the hearing who wanted to ask such questions. Major D. M. Owen, the lawyer who had been retained as counsel for the Indians, seems to have made more effort to defend Father Mackey than to represent his own clients. The *Truro Daily News* gave an account of Major Owen's summing up, "Almost Inconceivable says Major Owen in Summing up His Case. Investigation at Shubenacadie School is Concluded":

> Mr. Justice L.A. Audette's official enquiry into the flogging
> of 19 Indian youths at the reservation school here drew to a

close today as Major D.M. Owen, K.C., counsel for the Indians began summing up the evidence.

"If these allegations are found to be true, then Father Mackey is deserving of severe censure," declared Mr. Owen. He said he had known the principal of the school for 20 years and had always had great respect for him.

"But it is almost inconceivable to understand how after this service to church and humanity in the past he could have changed his procedure so suddenly," he continued.

When Judge Audette completed his report a little over three months later he completely exonerated and even praised Father Mackey. The *Halifax Herald* summarized Audette's conclusion:

Far from finding fault with the principal of the school for what he had done, he should be commended and congratulated for carefully investigating the conduct of his pupils and finding all the culprits and punishing them in a commensurate manner. How could order, discipline and good behaviour be maintained in the school if he were to have acted otherwise than he did? The punishment was quite reasonable and adequate under the circumstances and was in no way excessive.

Audette sprinkled his 54,000-word report with statements about his belief in the beneficial effects of physical punishment. The seventy-eight-year-old Judge reminisced happily about schooldays, "Where is the man who has gone to school in his boyhood and managed to get through without a taste of the strap? If he did, he must have been a true saint or a clever hypocrite who has been able to deceive his teachers." Audette also argued that, "All human governments rest, in the last resort upon physical pain," and suggested that the use of the strap, the cane and the birch in English schools had helped build the British Empire: "Reading the biography of the big men who moulded the destiny of the British nation, we invariably find a reference to these corrective punishments to which they were subjected in their school days." If the strap was good enough for the "big men" who built the British Empire then it was obviously good enough for Indians who,

Audette said, "are children having human minds just emerging from barbarism."

Two days later, The *Halifax Herald* carried an editorial expressing considerable satisfaction at the vindication of Father Mackey and making fun of the complaint against him.

Charges Unfounded

All small boys do not achieve the spotlight accorded a group of nineteen mischief-makers—a little worse—at Shubenacadie, and it is just as well for parental peace of mind. A Royal Commission has submitted a 54,000 word report on the punishment accorded these Indian youths caught telling untruths and involved in petty thievery. A judge of one of the highest courts of the country has investigated charges which, it turned out, were hastily made and wholly unfounded.

Had the commission decided the allegations of cruelty other than baseless, the case would not have had an amusing side. Imagine, however, a Crown inquiry every time a favourite son was punished for robbing a cookie jar with ensuing punishment—an investigation into his threats to become a pirate, a Buffalo Bill, or to die in spectacular martyrdom. Fortunately there need be no fear of such a situation arising. Youth's revolt has failed and the strap, the ruler and the birch retain their respected place in bolstering the solidity of the home, with the added benediction of a judge.

The Shubenacadie affair has its serious aspects as well. Teachers and others who serve in our schools and institutions will understand this. It is refreshing to find the hand of authority upheld when it is just. Adults must retain control, and how difficult this is, those with even a moderate-sized family can realize. At the same time it is reassuring to know that should there be a hint of cruelty or injustice in the institutions which the public supports there will be prompt investigation of the charges. Those administering the Dominion's school at Shubenacadie may continue their splendid work among the Indians of the Maritime Provinces certain of fullest support from a public which in cases of this kind never judges hastily.

No doubt, as far as the editorial writer was concerned, that was the end of the matter. But many questions remain unanswered. Judge Audette's report is missing from all the national archives and libraries. I have been told that there were probably seven copies originally. One of those seven copies was probably destroyed in the bonfire of the school's official records ordered by Father Collins. But copies would also have been deposited in the National Archives in Ottawa, the Department of Indian Affairs, and probably in the Parliamentary Library. A complete search of these and several other places which might have received a copy have failed to turn up any of the seven copies which once existed. Other evidence of what exactly took place at the school during the time of the March 1934 beating has also disappeared. The correspondence between Indian Affairs and Father Mackey during March and April of 1934 as well as the record of the formal complaint by Allison MacDonald, the Indian Agent, have also vanished because there is a four-month gap, from December 1933 to April 1934 in the Indian Affairs School file for Shubenacadie in the National Archives. Archivists acknowledge that this gap, along with the complete disappearance of the Audette Report, suggests that these documents have been destroyed. When and by whom? Judging from the attitudes expressed in the press reports, it seems unlikely that anyone in 1934 would have thought of Judge Audette's report as very controversial. If the report and the other evidence surrounding this event were deliberately destroyed, then it would almost certainly have been at a later date when public and political attitudes had begun to change.

One of the puzzling repeated references in the documents that are still available is to "a certain individual [who] is doing a lot of talking," mentioned in Father Mackey's letter to Indian Affairs about Matthew Thomas, the boy who had a kidney removed, and justifying himself against the implied charge of negligence. Judge Audette seems to make a similar reference in his report, as quoted in the *Halifax Herald,* to an attempt "to undermine the reputation of the institution, to make a storm in a tea cup, by spreading the false news that the strap had been dipped in vinegar before using it. The evidence abundantly establishes that it was absolutely false. There was a prejudicial and mischievous mind behind it all that endeavoured to hurt the school." If the person being referred to here was the Indian Agent Allison MacDonald, it seems unlikely that he would have been able to continue in his position in the face of a Federal Court Judge associating him with the criminal offence of "spreading false news." Or it may be that Indian Affairs recognized Audette's report as a necessary whitewash and knew that MacDonald's allegations against Father Mackey were all true. Whichever is the case, MacDonald continued to act as Indian Agent for the area for another two years. It is possible that the "certain individual who is doing a lot of talking" in Father Mackey's letter was Dr. D.F. McInnes, who was the School's attending physician. McInnes had written at least one letter to Indian Affairs complaining that the children at the school were neglected and ill-treated. Almost exactly a year before the Shubenacadie hearing, the doctor wrote to request "a thorough investigation" of the case of Josephine Smith who had died of peritonitis two days after collapsing in Mass. He angrily stated in his letter, "I don't consider the people in charge of an institution which would cause such negligence fit people to be in charge." Indian Affairs' "thorough investigation" seems to have consisted of writing to ask for Father Mackey's side of the story. They were apparently satisfied with his explanation that Josephine Smith had merely been "suffering . . . like a good many more from . . . the cold that was going around . . . We had no reason to think that her condition was any more serious than the others." That McInnes and Mackey had clashed is also suggested by the fact that one of the points on which Father Mackey was questioned in the hearing was whether he had attempted to prevent Dr. McInnes from coming to the school at the time of the thrashing.

The majority of the nineteen boys who were flogged are now dead, as are many of their 1934 classmates. In any case, what remains in the survivors' minds is the memory of the beating itself. As children they knew nothing of the political machinery which led first to a public hearing and then to the dismissal of all the allegations against Father Mackey. Also, at that time, many of their parents were unable to read and write, and therefore had to rely on people like my father to let them know what was in the newspapers.

I have heard one story which illustrates the effect the hearing had on the Native community. One man told me that his father was present at a Council meeting which took place in the fall of 1934, after

Audette's report had cleared Father Mackey of all wrongdoing. Two things shocked me when he told me his story. The first was that the special Council meeting was called in order to discuss a plan to assassinate Father Mackey. The second was that the man who had asked for the meeting to be called was my own father, John Knockwood, and it was held in my parents' house. They discussed what they knew of all the events which had led to the hearing and eventually reached the agreement that the only way justice could be done was through their own actions and that Father Mackey would have to be killed. I was told that my father then cut sticks of different lengths and they used them to choose the man who would have to act as executioner. They sat for a long time in silence after each pulled a stick, so no one yet knew if he had chosen the shortest. [One elder with whom I discussed this story suggested that the sticks would have been all the same length since Mi'kmaw traditions would deem all of them equally involved in the decision.]

Eventually one elder began to speak. He spoke of the frustration of being unable to help the children at the school now that there was nothing to prevent Father Mackey and Edward McLeod from strapping them just as savagely as they had beaten the nineteen boys in March. Even if these beatings became public, it seemed that any court would not only find him innocent but would praise him for what he had done. Then he asked, but what will happen to the children in those locked dormitories after we kill Father Mackey? This began a long discussion about the consequences for the children if Father Mackey was killed. Surely they would be in even greater danger. After talking nearly all night the men agreed that killing Father Mackey would only endanger the children's lives still further and that the only way they could protect children at the school was to make sure they visited on every available occasion. Then, one by one, the men rose and burnt their sticks in the Council fire.

Although Chief John Maloney, my father, and the other men who met that night were nearly powerless in their attempt to see justice done and to protect their children, the consequences of the 1934 beating and of other brutal punishments at the school continued to be felt for many decades. By the 1960s, Native leaders were beginning to formulate their own policy on education which led later on to the National Indian Brotherhood's 1972 statement on Indian Control of

Indian Education. Many meetings and many hours and days of discussion led up to the development of that policy. At one of those meetings a man made a very powerful argument for our taking full control of our children's education. No one remembers exactly what Edward Poulette said, but everyone who was there remembers what he did. He took off his shirt and showed the scars on his back. They had been put there over thirty years earlier by Edward McLeod and Father Mackey.

CHAPTER 9

OUT OF THE DEPTHS

Please don't blame yourselves for what happened at the Indian Residential Schools, for the Great Spirit's sake, we were only children.

Scared and frightened children who were taken hundreds of miles away from home. We were beaten to learn and live a different life and culture, children who were forced to speak English and Latin instead of Micmac.

It's time to be heard by the people of Canada. Only the ones who went to the Indian Schools know what went on because we lived it. We've lived it every day of our lives.

—*Imelda Brooks, Big Cove, N.B.*
Micmac-Maliseet News, May 1991.

How can you forget your past? It's a part of your thoughts every day. This is our history and now we're talking about it.
—*Rita Howe*

Every one of the students who attended the Indian Residential School in Shubenacadie during the nearly forty years it was open has their own story to tell. Some say, "Thank God for the Residential School" and that they learned valuable skills such as how to speak English, how to keep themselves and their homes clean, and how to sew and cook, and especially how to pray. Some of these people deny there were any beatings, while others say that the beatings were deserved and justified. Among this group were children who were "good" themselves or else had bigger sisters and brothers to look after them. Others were priests' and nuns' pets and favourites who were used as spies. Some looked on the school as a refuge from homes where they were abused, frequently by parents who had themselves attended the school and learned physical punishment as a method of child-rearing.

On the other hand many former students say that the Residential School was a terrible childhood experience and tell shocking stories of what happened to them there. Yet they all seem to make an effort to understand what motivated the priests and nuns who ran the school. "I've tried to understand why the priests and nuns acted the way they did toward us and I can't justify any of the beatings no matter how much I try," a former student, who is now a grandmother, told me.

Nearly everyone had many difficulties when they left the school finding an identity and a place in the world. Some went home to the reserves after being discharged from the school only to find out that they didn't fit in, and when they tried to point out the social ills at home were told, "You don't belong here. Go back to where you came from." Even those of us who had parents who welcomed us home were suspended in limbo because we could no longer speak Mi'kmaw.

Despite school years where religion was practised as brutal compulsion some former students still persist in endless churchgoing and expect God to come and solve everything. Others have become addicted to gambling in the false hope of becoming rich. Many others are staying home, collecting welfare instead of earning wages, because there are no jobs on the Reserves. We have too many who are living in perpetual bliss under the influence of drugs and alcohol, thus becoming numb to the real problems and their practical solutions. However, others have claimed as adults the education they were denied as children. One person who has started on this path told me her reason for this: "The same treatment I suffered at the Resi will never again be inflicted on Native people."

These people include counsellors like Nora Bernard, who have examined their lives and traced patterns which developed in childhood. Nora realized that her alcoholism began with drinking altar wine while she was a teenager at the school serving as an altar girl. She is now a counsellor for the Native Alcohol and Drug Addiction Center. She says, "I had to experience all this in order to do the work that I have chosen."

Several former students have told me that one of the the school's most devastating effects on their lives is that it instilled a fear of touching or of being physically close to other people. When Georgina Denny went to live at Eskasoni after spending her entire childhood at the school she says that she was "fascinated" by the way people would show physical affection, "Everybody else seemed like they were so loving—holding and touching—I couldn't even have anyone sit next to me close." Another woman I talked to traced back her fear of touching to an incident at the school and the lessons instilled there:

> When I crawled in my sister's bed during a thunderstorm to keep warm, the Sister came along checking the beds and found me and my sister. I was cuddled up next to my sister and she said that we weren't allowed to sleep together because it's not clean to sleep with someone. They taught us to stay away and not be touching. It's a natural thing to touch someone you love, be it your sister, brother, mother, father. It was pure innocence, real love. And they pushed that away from us and told us that it was dirty . . . Today I have a hard time. I don't want anybody to touch me unless I'm really close to them. I even have a hard time shaking hands. I want to be close to my family, but they're like me, afraid to hug me. The closest thing they ever tell me is, "See you tomorrow."

Her mother had also been a student at the school and she has no recollection of ever being hugged as a child. She speculates that her mother's refusal to touch her children was taught at the school, but she herself has deliberately changed the way she treats her own child. "I broke that cycle of not touching. I hug my daughter and tell her all the time that I love her."

Those who ran the school tried to rob us of our collective identity by punishing us for speaking our language, calling us "savages" and "heathens." They also tried to take away our individual identities. Often the nuns would arbitrarily change a child's name. Margaret Knockwood remembers, "Sister wrote 'Marjorie' on the board and told me, 'Your name is not Margaret. It's Marjorie.' So I was known as Marjorie at the school." Another girl named Margaret was also re-named by the nuns. We had all been forced to call Margaret Julian "Peggy O'Neill." She had been so constantly punished at school that I somehow assumed that she must have died. But thirty years later I met her. "Oh, Peggy, I thought they had killed you." She replied, "No, almost. But I'm Margaret Julian remember? It's Johnson now." She had taken back her real name and identity and built another life on it as a married woman.

Strangely enough, some of the students who were most seriously abused have been able to transform their lives and bring themselves "out of the depths." Wallis LeBillois ran away in 1939 and was hounded down by a police dog. He grew up to become a political activist, spending some of his time helping the National Indian Brotherhood, now the Assembly of First Nations (AFN), develop its policy on Native education and eventually become Elder-in-Residence for the AFN.

Others have claimed their own identity and the meaning of their lives through the rediscovery of Native spiritual traditions. Despite the efforts of those who ran the school to instill hatred and contempt for Native traditions and culture, many of us have returned to a traditional path as the the source of our strength. One man I interviewed joked that he now describes himself as "a born-again savage." Some of us have come to realize that we were abused not only physically but spiritually. For us, the Native Way with its Sacred Circle and respect for all living things is a means of healing that abuse.

The Talking Stick has come full circle. When Sister Mary Leonard told us that the Catholic Church believed in the saying, "Give me a child before the age of seven, and I will show you the adult," she was speaking a larger truth than she knew. Many years will have to pass before the damage inflicted by the Residential School can be healed. I am still dealing with the mentally, emotionally and spiritually damaged child of five. It makes me angry that the people who almost destroyed me got away with it because they grew old and died before I could confront them. My anger led to frustration because there is nothing I could do to even things up. I cannot confront those who lied to me about myself and about my people and withheld knowledge from me which could have allowed me to live up to my fullest potential. It made no real difference that government officials and some representatives of the Catholic church apologized to Native people for the schools. Those individuals who directly caused our suffering never admitted their wrongdoing and were never called to account for their actions.

My path has taken many twists and turns which eventually led to the writing of this book. Long before I began writing it, Sulian Herney, my mentor at Mi'kmaw Lodge, had counselled me by saying, "Isabelle the adult has to go back into that school and find Isabelle the child, and take her by the hand and get her out of there." I have done that, and I find myself in a safer place where people are willing to listen, which is the first step of the healing process.

There is one story which I have not fully told till now. Two days before the derelict school burned down, when I went there with my daughter and granddaughter, they went ahead of me up the steps and stopped suddenly. They had heard a voice from behind the half-open door whisper, "Come in, you're welcome." My mother, Deodis, had always talked out loud to ghosts or spirits when she felt their presence. "Who's there?" I called out. "Is that you Father Mackey? Is that you Sister Superior? Show yourself." There was no answer, but I shouted back. "You got me when I was a child. But I'm here now and you can't have my children and my grandchildren."

I pass the Talking Stick to you.